GROWING FROM WORD PLAY INTO POETRY

by Buff Bradley
with the editors of LEARNING Magazine

LEARNING Handbooks
530 University Avenue
Palo Alto, California 94301

FOREWORD

The classroom-tested activities in this handbook range from making things with art materials and words to playing word games to exploring abstract poetic forms. This broad mix of strategies puts children at ease while they develop skills for writing and understanding poetry.

The purpose of this and other LEARNING Handbooks is to help make teaching and learning more effective, interesting and exciting. Buff Bradley is a poet and former teacher who has led creative writing workshops in elementary and secondary schools. His extensive experience has been combined with LEARNING magazine's research facilities and editorial depth to produce this down-to-earth and lively handbook.

EDITOR: Carol B. Whiteley
DESIGNER: David Hale
ILLUSTRATIONS: Dennis Ziemienski
COVER: Robert G. Bryant

EXECUTIVE EDITOR: Roberta Suid
EDITORIAL DIRECTOR: Morton Malkofsky
DESIGN DIRECTOR: Robert G. Bryant

Library of Congress Number: 76-29235
International Standard Book Number: 0-915092-09-3

Book Code: 011 • First Printing October 1976

CONTENTS

PROLOGUE

4

PART ONE

Introduction 8

Making Things With Words 12

Playing With Words 32

PART TWO

Introduction 54

Using the Poet's Tools 57

Looking for Poems 75

EPILOGUE

90

RESOURCES

92

PROLOGUE

Play is the earnest and immense business of the child, growing himself or herself into the world. Running, skipping, jumping and climbing all help to build muscles and develop motor skills. Playing games and working puzzles nurture organized thinking and promote eye-hand coordination. As children play together they learn about rules, about themselves and about communication. It's pretty evident that the real work of childhood is play.

As kids grow into verbal language, they play games with new toys—words. Nursery rhymes are really word games and sound games, things that are fun to say and fun to hear. They exist not for meaning but for pure language:

> Hey Diddle-diddle
> The cat and the fiddle
> The cow jumped over the moon
> The little dog laughed
> To see such sport
> And the dish ran away with the spoon

Many nursery rhymes may once have "meant" something—for example, "Hey Diddle-diddle" may have been written as a collection of picturesque English tavern and inn names. But any meanings that such rhymes might have had are lost for young children today, and what remains are the delightfully nonsensical words and sounds that make them fun to say and hear.

Word play doesn't begin and end with nursery rhymes; kids play with words and sounds constantly. A little girl counts to ten, beginning every number with the letter "b"—bun, boo, bree, bour, bive, bix, beven, beight, bine, ben. A boy entertains himself for a few minutes by saying all the words he can think of that rhyme with "me"—see, knee, tree, bee, we, pee, she, key—and when he runs out of words he knows, he keeps on going—chee, stee, jee, pree, kwee, ree.

In her book *Learn to Read, Read to Learn,* Beatrice Landeck tells how a group of girls made up a whole new version of the traditional black song "Hush Little Baby" while they were skipping rope. Once they start substituting new rhymes for old, she says, "the rhyming is as much fun as the rope skipping, each child trying to outdo the other. The game is repeated with the new verses that are more fun in play than the traditional ones. After a few repetitions, all the children on the block are substituting the new lyric for the old. Versifying for the pure joy of sound and rhythm is a natural and appropriate way for children to express themselves."

As kids grow into language, they start to play with meanings as well as with sounds and rhythms. They exult in nonsense, in calling things by the wrong name: the giraffe ate the sky; the refrigerator sneezed; my daddy is a carrot; the turkey said bow-wow; the sidewalk laughed at me; I can't go to bed until I put on my bananas. In some of his poems, though they go far deeper than children's spontaneous amusements, Theodore Roethke tapped into the sense and the sound of this kind of word playing:

> I know her noise.
> Her neck has kittens.
> I'll make a hole for her.
> In the fire.[1]

Childhood is not one universe but the confluence of many—the Self, the Other, Body, Thought, Family, Imagination and on and on. One of those universes is Language, and the child explores it as he does all the others—through play.

There are quite a few people who tell us that kids are natural poets. The proof, they say, is the freshness of their language, the vividness of their imagery, the spontaneity of their expressions. Three-year-old Danny, dressing himself, put on a pair of pants first. Then, trying to decide which shirt to wear, he held one next to his pants and asked, "Do these rhyme, Mommy?" Though no poet would ever deny the value of "accidental" discoveries or happen-

---

[1]From "Where Knock is Wide Open."

ings in his or her work, poetry is more than accident or serendipity. No matter how vivid Danny's image is, he didn't *mean* rhyme, his intention wasn't to say something startlingly new and original. Rhyming shirts and pants are a charming thought, but the expression simply wasn't a thought-out conception.

To produce a poem, the poet must conceive, plan and execute. The good poem most often happens by design—the poet calculates meanings, orchestrates various elements and works to achieve an effect. The ability to do all this comprises a complex of skills, and these skills must be learned, perhaps even taught. (The concepts of "talent" and "genius" are of no use here. They are *ex post facto* terms—we look at a poem and after reading it say, "It shows real genius" or "The poet is highly talented." Even if the ethereal qualities of talent and genius do exist—a dubious proposition at best—any discussion of them in the context of teaching poetry still misses the point, because they can only be manifested in good poems, and *writing good poems takes definite skills*.)

When you come upon a particularly well-coordinated three-year-old, you don't drag her over to try out for the neighborhood soccer team. You wait. You let her grow. You encourage and nurture her physical development. Someday, when the time is right, she *may* play soccer. And however much your four-year-old son loves music, you know that four years old is normally too young to start formal music lessons (all cries of "Mozart" hereby acknowledged). You wait. You sing with him. You buy him records. And someday, maybe . . . .

It is the same with poetry. Just because a young child likes to fiddle and experiment with all sorts of words, you don't plop her down in the middle of sestinas and similes. You encourage her word play, help direct it with different games and activities and nurture the development of her abilities with lively and unusual language experiences.

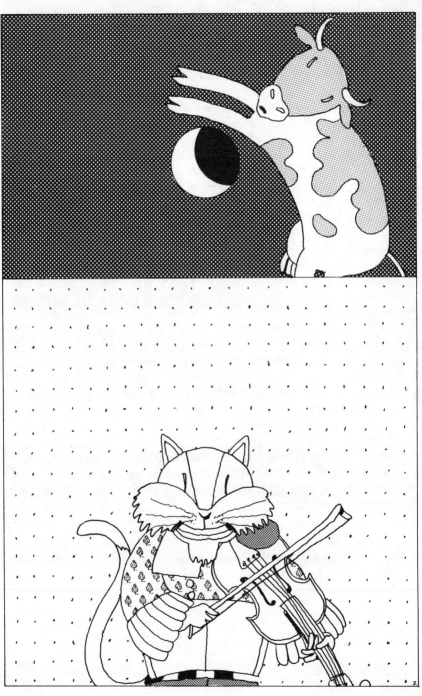

PART ONE

Introduction

The first half of this book is about playing with words: the first chapter involves concrete experiences—making things with art materials and words—and the second chapter is more abstract—playing word games. The second half of the book works with writing and learning about poetry: the third chapter gets kids writing poems and exploring the tools and skills the poet works with, and the fourth chapter explores various poetic forms. The word play activities and chapters can be seen as preparation for the poetry. Besides promoting language development, their aim is to help make kids more at ease with, and more responsive to, the special kind of writing poetry is, with its images, its metaphors, its unusual juxtapositions of words, its rhythms, alliterations and onomatopoeias. The poem-making activities intend to teach kids how the poet works and what the poet makes. Most of the activities in both sections are ones the author has used successfully in various classrooms. The rest come from other poets and writing teachers and have worked well for them in their classes.

At what point, you may be thinking, do you stop the word play and start in on the poetry? The answer to the first half of the question is "never." Though their games may be different from children's, all writers are word players. Even when your classroom writers are producing real poems, they ought to go back to word play from time to time. It'll get their poetic juices flowing; they may make discoveries they can use in their poems; and, in addition, they'll have lots of fun.

The answer to the second half of the question comes less quickly. Formal poetry really is a kind of sustained expression, and very young children are less likely to be able to "hold onto" the sense of what they're trying to write about. Also, poems, except for silly nonsense poems and sing-songy rhymes, may not interest them very much. Older children are more likely to be able to get down and work at the essence of what they're trying to say. And their increasing sophistication—about themselves, about the world, about language and literature—probably will make them more interested in, and more responsive to, poetic forms. These observations, however, are simply working suggestions. You know your students' abilities and responsiveness best; when you think they're ready, try a few activities from the second half of the book. If they prove too difficult or demanding, go back to word play, and try the poetry activities again at a later date.

It is not necessary for you to do the activities in the order in which they're presented. You and your class can choose freely among the activities, and, ideally, they will generate variations and even brand-new activities for you to try. Used occasionally, any of the activities can be lots of fun for kids; used regularly, however, they can be more than fun—they can help get kids deeply and joyfully involved in the world of words and the world of poetry. Daily work with an activity is ideal, but use them as your time and schedule permit. For younger kids doing word play activities, a half-hour is usually long enough. The poetry-writing exercises, however, are likely to demand more time and an hour may prove to be a good limit. Spending more than an hour on one poetry activity may dissipate the interest and energy of young writers.

If you want to help children learn to write poetry, there's nothing you can do for them that's more important than *reading them poems*. Part of every writing class, from the first day on, ought to be given to reading some poems—one or two each period—to children. The poetry you read ought to be a mix of poems written by and/or for children, and serious "adult" poetry—you'll find there's plenty of adult poetry that kids can relate to. (The resource section at the end of this book lists several collections of poems from which you can choose.)

In the beginning, unless some kids have something they want to say, it is enough just to read the poems with little or no comment—one of the surest ways to ruin good poetry for children is to lecture on it. But as the kids get more involved in making poems, and as their sense of what poetry is grows, you can try generating discussions about what you're reading to your class, relating those poems to the skills, techniques and kinds of poems the kids are working with themselves. Still, the poem's the thing, and if discussions are deadly or difficult, they ought to be dropped and the poetry should be allowed to speak for itself. Exposure to good poems, even in small doses, can do more than all the lectures and activities in the world to develop taste and judgment and a true and deep appreciation of poetry.

Enthusiasm, too, can promote interest in poetry—no matter how exciting any poetry activity seems to be, it can be a thumping bore if your enthusiasm for the subject is missing. If you don't know much about or care for poetry yourself, it will be difficult to generate excitement about it. But hopefully you like poetry, and plan to learn more about it along with your students. It will make a big difference to you and your class if, instead of just leading the writing activities in this book, you do them right along with the kids, sharing the experience in every way.

Making Things With Words

Kids like to make things—they like to color and paint and cut and paste and mold and draw and staple. The knowledgeable art teacher will give kids bunches of materials and a bit of guidance, and set the children loose to explore the possibilities of the media. If kids don't feel forced to *produce*, their work will be free and exuberant, and in the doing they will learn all sorts of things about what they can do and what they like to do.

Just as paper, paint, crayons and glue are the raw materials the young artist plays with and explores to develop his abilities, so are words the young poet's raw materials; as the artist learns by playing with the tools of his craft, the poet can learn through unconfined play with his "materials" without the need for "sense" or "meaning." (Some grown-up writers don't put too much stock in the notion of "meaning" either. Archibald MacLeish wrote in his well-known *Ars Poetica*, "A poem should not mean, but be.")

The analogy between the beginning artistic process and the beginning poetic process can be put to work easily and naturally by including words in the process of making things. (The Greek root word for "poem" is "poiein"—to make.) In this way, words can become parts of objects—in a sense, more concrete, less abstract. Making words the key ingredient for making objects is a graceful, effective way to tap into children's natural delight with manipulating materials and creating pretty things.

Poets are always looking for new and unusual ways of saying things, of making images and of quickening language so it will have force and impact. The first, third and tenth activities in this chapter are all about making and discovering images through more

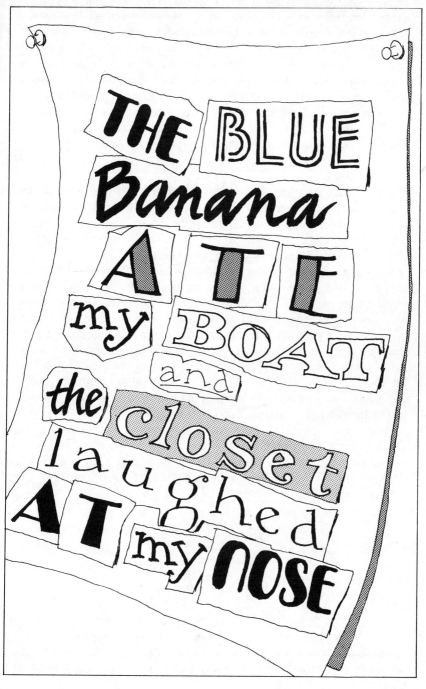

THE BLUE Banana ATE my BOAT and the closet laughed AT my NOSE

13

or less random juxtapositions of words. They are really concrete externalizations of what goes on inside the poet all the time—fitting words together, experimenting with every sort of combination. The fourth and fifth activities have kids explore two poetic conventions, rhyme and alliteration. Most modern poets have abandoned heavy reliance on rhyming, but alliteration in contemporary poems is quite common. The second, sixth, seventh, eighth and twelfth activities ask kids to illustrate or interpret words or poems with visual images. And in the other two activities, the children celebrate words by wearing them.

Word Poster

It's easy to fill up your classroom with words and poems by filling it up with word/poem posters. One word poster kids can make is simply that—a large piece of poster board or construction paper filled with words. It's particularly good for beginning readers—they can use their posters to practice reading.

Kids can make the posters by writing their own words on scraps of paper—the more colors of paper they use, the brighter and livelier the posters will be. With crayons or felt pens, kids can write as many words as they want, putting only one word on each scrap of paper; then they can cut the scraps into various shapes and glue them onto the poster in any way they like. Some students may want their posters to have themes—animal names, food names and so on. Others may wish to cut words or single letters from old newspapers and magazines they bring in to class, and glue those, instead of the hand-written scraps, to the cardboard.

Another poster kids can make is a "Crazy Poem" poster, using random word combinations. It's best if the whole class works together to make the first poster. Start them out by showing them a "crazy" nonsense poem you've made yourself, on the order of the one below:

The blue banana
ate
my boat
and the closet
laughed at my nose

Equip the kids with pencils, crayons, pens, scissors and scraps of paper. (You will need some poster board and glue.) Have them write two or more words, one word per scrap, to correspond with words in the model poem (to speed things up you might want to provide the articles, conjunctions, prepositions, etc., yourself.) For example, you might ask the kids to write the names of two different colors; two fruits or vegetables; two verbs; two places or rooms in a house; two articles of clothing; two more verbs; two parts of the body. Once the words have been written down, get a large poster board or piece of construction paper and put it where everyone can see it. Glue a "the" into place, then ask for a color word from someone, a fruit or vegetable name from someone else, then a verb and so on, building the poem on the poster. After the whole class has collaborated on the first one, have kids use it as a model and make crazy poems of their own with their remaining words or with new words they write on other scraps. (As with the first poster, the kids can use words and letters cut from magazines and newspapers instead of writing words on paper scraps. One group of fourth graders added an extra dimension to their posters by cutting out the sections of egg cartons, gluing individual words inside each section, painting them with tempera, then attaching them to poster board.) The children can share their poems by displaying the posters on walls and bulletin boards.

Word Collages

The collage is an art activity standby—it involves cutting images or shapes from magazines and newspapers and gluing them in various arrangements onto construction paper. Kids can make a new kind of collage by using letters and words instead of pictures and forms, or they may combine words with pictures to add even greater interest.

Your class can start out by making a standard picture collage. Once the pictures are glued into place, have the kids look through magazines and newspapers for words that identify the pictures (chair, horse, etc.) or words that describe the pictures (yellow, ugly, etc.). If they can't find the words they want, they can make them by cutting out individual letters, using a variety of typefaces and sizes. When the kids glue on the words, they can play it straight by attaching appropriate words to appropriate pictures—the word "turkey" onto a picture of a turkey, "delicious" onto a piece of pie or an ice cream cone—or they can fool around and mix everything up, sticking "cantaloupe" onto a Volkswagen and "Volkswagen" onto a piano. They can also use their cut-out words to make a comment—"awful" on a can of spinach, or "cough" on a package of cigarettes.

Another kind of collage uses only words—again, words cut out as a whole, or words made of individual cut-out letters. In the

15

collage, the words aren't arranged randomly, but are placed in such a way that they create a particular image. For a flower collage, kids might start by picking such words as "flower," "grow," "green," "leaf," "red" and "pretty," cut them out and then glue them onto a poster in the shape of a flower, as the accompanying drawing illustrates. For an airplane collage they could use "wing," "jet," "fly," "high" and "fast" and form them into a plane.

Another variation on the theme can involve more than a single image—kids can use word collages to create a whole scene. They can use words alone, or they can combine words and pictures to create a really exciting masterpiece.

Instead of putting their collages onto construction paper or poster board, kids can also decoupage them. This process involves gluing images and words to a sturdy surface and then covering the entire creation with another coat of glue. The decoupage can be made on a piece of wood or a piece of cardboard. (If wood is used, the surface must be sanded smooth.) Once the pictures and words are cut out, kids should prepare a mixture of white glue and water, making it about the thickness of cream. Have them spread the glue mixture onto the surface, then stick the words and pictures they've cut out in place. Then they should cover the entire surface—the wood or cardboard and the cut-outs—with the glue mixture—it will dry clear, with a shiny finish.

Word Mobiles

Most kids love to make their own mobiles, with cut-out pictures and shapes, bits of junk, twigs, shells, pine cones or whatever is handy. They can make mobiles using words, too.

To start, each child will need five equal lengths of small dowels or sticks, cardboard, some string, strong thread or nylon fishing line, scissors and glue. At first it's best to help the kids keep their mobiles symmetrical so that they'll balance properly and hang right. (The one on page 19 is a good one to use as an example.) Later kids can experiment with asymmetrical arrangements.

Have the kids cut out 16 squares of cardboard all the same size (about 3 inches by 3 inches) and use a hole punch or scissors' points to make holes in them near the top edge at the center. Then have each child cut five 8-inch lengths of string and 16 5-inch lengths. Ask them to tie their dowels together (as shown in the drawing on page 19) with the 8-inch lengths of string. Then they should tie one of the 5-inch strings onto each cardboard square. Before they assemble their mobiles by tying the squares to the dowels, most kids will probably want to glue pictures, words

and letters onto the squares. They can use words and pictures as they were used in the preceding activity, first cutting out pictures and gluing them onto the cardboard squares, and then cutting out words to glue onto the pictures. (The words may be appropriate, wholly inappropriate, or make comments.) Or they can make a "Crazy Poem Mobile," with one word written or glued onto each cardboard square. As in the first activity, you will probably want the first mobile to be a class effort, and will want to use a model, such as this one:

> The sleepy truck
> sneezed horses
> into my green yawn
> and they galloped
> 100 inches
> to lunch

To make a crazy poem mobile, ask the kids to write on scraps of paper or cut from magazines and newspapers the following or similar words: two "the's," two "feeling" adjectives (happy, angry, frightened, etc.), two animal names and so on. When this is done, have the class collaborate on one crazy poem with various kids contributing the words you call for. Glue the words onto the 3-inch by 3-inch cardboard squares, and then assemble and hang for all to see. This mobile can serve as a model for kids to use in making their own. They might want to try making a mobile of a short poem, sentence or message, using individual letters of various colors, typefaces and sizes cut from magazines and newspapers. (See the illustration on p. 19.)

Kids can also make mobiles with balloons instead of cardboard squares, using felt-tipped pens or ball-point pens to write their words onto the balloons. (Ball-points seem to work best if you use them on the balloons before they're blown up. Kids who have trouble writing small should blow up balloons first, though, and then write on them with felt pens.)

Chains

Paper chains are good, cheap decorations for parties and Christmas trees, and they also make an appealing medium with which kids can collect words. Chains can be made by cutting out 1- by 6-inch strips of various colors of construction paper, gluing the ends of one strip together to form a circle, looping the next strip through it and gluing its ends together, and so on.

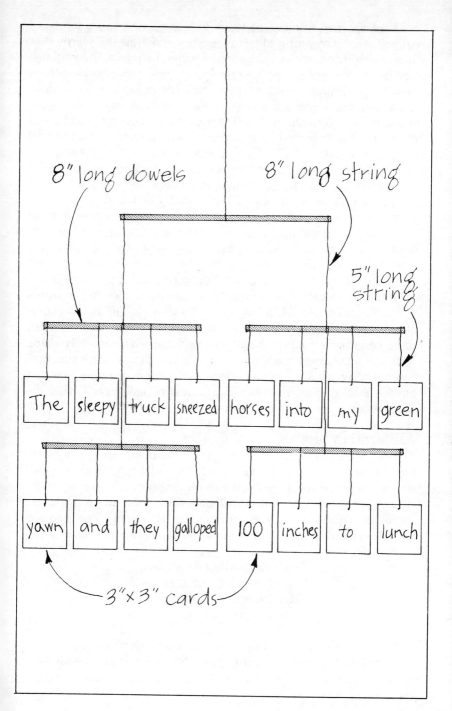

8" long dowels

8" long string

5" long string

The | sleepy | truck | sneezed | horses | into | my | green

yawn | and | they | galloped | 100 | inches | to | lunch

3"×3" cards

There are any number of ways to use paper chains for word collections. Very young kids can simply write all the words that they can think of, one on each strip of paper, then form their chains. You can use the chains to decorate your classroom, hanging them from the ceiling or attaching them to bulletin boards. Each child can add to his or her chain at a special time every day, every week or whenever. Word chains are also good for collecting special kinds of words—the kids could make noun chains, adverb chains, animal name chains, slang chains. Particularly useful for "could-be" poets are word chains that gather words related to poetic conventions— alliteration chains, rhyme chains, onomatopoeia chains.

Kids can make word chains individually or together as a class project. For individual chains, each kid can pick a rhyme word ("tree") or a beginning sound or letter ("y") and make his or her own chain, continually adding a rhyming word or word that begins with the chosen sound or letter. Whole-class chains can be made using a wall or a bulletin board, labeling each category at the top of the chain ("A Chain," "B Chain," "C Chain," etc., for all the letters of the alphabet) and letting anyone who wants to add to the chains at appropriate times. Kids should read all the words on the chains to be certain their additions don't duplicate what's already there. You can encourage students to go to the dictionary once they run out of words they're familiar with. There might be a rule that anyone adding a word to the chain must be able to tell what the word means.

Alliteration Stories

The little girl in the introduction to this handbook who counted to ten beginning all the numbers with "b"—"bun," "boo," "bree," etc.—was using her own brand of alliteration. Alliteration is an old, old poetic device, but even today, poets who might never use rhyme or regular meter keep alliteration in their workbags to use for achieving a special kind of music, as Dylan Thomas does here:

> This day winding down now
> At God speeded summer's end
> In the torrent salmon sun
> In my seashaken house . . . .[1]

The preceding activity suggests making alliteration chains. This activity asks kids to write alliteration stories. (All that's needed are

[1]From "Author's Prologue."

paper and pencils or pens.) One alliteration story can be built around a single letter—"A," for example—with the story containing as many words as possible that begin with that letter. (Depending on their abilities, kids can write anywhere from a few sentences to a few paragraphs.) Since the stories are fun to write but may not be easy, you'll probably want to provide your students with a model, such as this one:

> Albert and Alice ate all the apples at Aunt Amanda's. After they ate all the apples, Alice and Albert asked Aunt Amanda for apricots and animal crackers and ate all of them also. "Amazing!" cried Aunt Amanda. "Albert and Alice have awfully big appetites. All my apples and apricots and animal crackers are gone." After awhile, Alice and Albert went away. "At last!" said Aunt Amanda.

When the students run out of words they're familiar with, send them to hunt through the dictionary—it's a good way for them to expand their vocabularies. If you let them stretch things a bit by stuffing in a lot of extra words and using not-quite-correct sentence construction, kids will probably enjoy this activity more than if they have to be letter perfect.

Another alliteration story activity asks kids to write sentences that contain 2- or 3-word alliterative combinations using as many different letters as possible, rather than using words that begin with the same letter:

> Arnold asked Amy if she would bring brown bags to carry candy canes to Patrick's parents' party.

Older kids might be challenged to use all the letters of the alphabet in these alliteration stories.

Word Drawings
The point of this activity is for kids to consider the meanings of certain words—common words like "how," "where," "because," "my," but not concrete nouns that can be readily depicted in drawings—and to use those words as central images or figures in paintings or drawings that work to create visual understandings of what the words mean. (The drawings on page 22 provide the models for this activity.) There are several cartoonists who work with this format, particularly the American artist Saul Steinberg, who

does it brilliantly, often combining profound expression with high good humor. You might want to show some of his drawings to your class.

When you first use this activity, particularly with younger kids, it's good to use pairs of prepositional opposites, like over-under, on-off, up-down, in-out. In these word drawings, the meaning will depend on the relative positions of the words on paper. Gradually, kids can work up to more difficult and abstract words—"power," "can't," "understand" and the like. There is no success or failure, no right or wrong way to make the drawings. The activity is really a brain stretcher, an effort to combine a visual sense with the more complicated cerebral notion of "meaning."

Encourage your kids to design their words and pictures, in effect to design their own brand-new typefaces rather than settling for plain printing or cursive writing. In fact, a good complement to this activity is a study of typefaces and various kinds of calligraphy. Commercial typesetters, print shops and paper companies often have posters displaying different typefaces. They're an excellent resource, generally not too expensive, sometimes even free. A calligraphy demonstration can add interest to this activity, but calligraphers are not necessarily easy to find. Good places to start the search are art schools, advertising agencies and sign painting businesses.

Word Cards

Kids will quite likely want to keep some of the poems they make, some of the new words they learn and some of the pictures they draw during the course of their word play activities. One of the ways they can collect what they want to keep is, of course, in homemade books. Each child can collect pages of the material he has made and particularly fancies throughout the course of a school year, and can bind those pages together periodically to make his own personal books.

Books are pretty impressive, no doubt about it, and carry a kind of grown-up sense of accomplishment. But word cards, a kind of hybrid of flash cards and bubble-gum trading cards, may be more of the stuff of modern American childhood. Word cards may even turn more kids on to the idea of collecting and sharing—even trading—what they've made and discovered through word play.

Standard 3-inch by 5-inch index cards work well for making the word cards. Younger kids will probably have trouble writing and drawing on anything smaller; older kids might want to trim the cards down to bona fide trading card size. Using felt-tipped marking pens, kids can reproduce any poems, drawings, short paragraphs, etc., they want on the cards. (Kids might also keep new words they learn on these cards, with pictures on one side, definitions on the other.) First, have them draw a line down the middle of the card, separating it into two 3- by 2½-inch sections. On the left-hand side they can write their poem or story or word; on the right-hand side, they can make relevant drawings. If they wish to, the kids can write their names and some information about their work on the back of the cards—made by the poem computer, made for a mobile, an alliteration story, or whatever. Some kids have used these cards for postcards to send to friends, uncles and aunts, grandma and grandpa. They save the back for addresses, personal messages and a stamp.

Illustrating Poems

The sixth activity in this chapter suggests one way that the poet and the visual artist can come together. The drawing on the cover of this book is an example of another way. No matter how you do it, illustrating a poem is more than just another art activity; it is a way to get inside a poem, a way to see and understand it. It's a good, natural way to give kids a chance to learn what poems are about instead of only discussing the "meaning" with them.

On one level, illustrations of poems may be picture-stories. They may simply show what happens in the poem—the cow jumping over the moon, the blackbird snipping off a nose. Another level of illustration shows what happens in the poem and uses abstract imagery as well. The cover of this book is a good example of this second level: To picture "musics," the artist used bars and notes of musical notation. He also needed to show some abstraction—"musics" is not a verb, like "run" or "dance" or "smile," that can be depicted literally. We don't know what "musicking" looks like so we have to interpret. Interpreting is what illustrating poems is all about.

A third level, or mode, of poem illustrating is wholly unliteral. Instead of showing what happens in the poem, the artist tries to capture the central sense, mood or tone of the poem in his drawing.

Using the drawing on the cover as a model for your kids to study, ask your class to illustrate poems in one or all of the ways just described. They can use poems that have come from the class, poems you may read to them or favorite poems they may bring in. (Ask the children, especially if they bring in poems, to choose those that lend themselves to literal, informational drawings and abstract, or "interpretational," drawings.) Shorter poems in which something happens and in which there is an easily discernible mood or tone—sad, lonesome, joyful—are best. Once kids have completed their drawings, discussing the poem might well come more easily.

Word Shirts

Beethoven is celebrated on sweatshirts, Mickey Mouse on T-shirts—why not celebrate words and poems in the same way? Since kids wear smocks or Dad's old shirts for finger painting and clay modeling, why shouldn't they wear their own word shirts at word play time? It's becoming more and more popular for people to decorate their own clothes, and there are products available for decorating fabrics that are inexpensive, easy to use and un-messy enough to be practical for use in the classroom. The products, such as "Sharpie," "El Marko" and "Deco-write," won't run or smear on cloth; most hobby shops stock them.

A few days before you plan to make word shirts, ask each child to bring in a plain white or other solid color T-shirt in his or her proper size. They may also want to bring in some old shirts or scraps of cloth to practice on. (You might want to have extra scraps handy.) Before kids do a "final draft" on the shirts they want to keep, help them to practice on the old shirts or scraps.

Kids can word their shirts in any number of ways. They might want to use stencils to make the shirts properly spiffy. They could write one of the poems they make in another activity on the front and do a drawing on the back. They could pick one brand-new word as they do for the word badges in the eleventh activity and emblazon it across the chest. Perhaps they'd like to fill up a whole shirt with rhyming words or alliteration words; they could even write one of their alliteration stories on it. However kids choose to do it, making word shirts is a fun way to celebrate the kinds of things they are doing with language, and to make words part of what they enjoy and care about.

Word Blocks

Before "Sesame Street" came along, generations of children learned the alphabet (more or less) with alphabet blocks. Kids can make their own sets of word blocks and explore all sorts of word combinations while playing with them.

Word blocks can be well-sanded scraps of wood, or they can be pieces of lightweight cardboard. Each cardboard block uses two 3-by 9-inch strips of cardboard, and each strip is divided into three 3-by 3-inch squares and folded as shown in the accompanying illus-

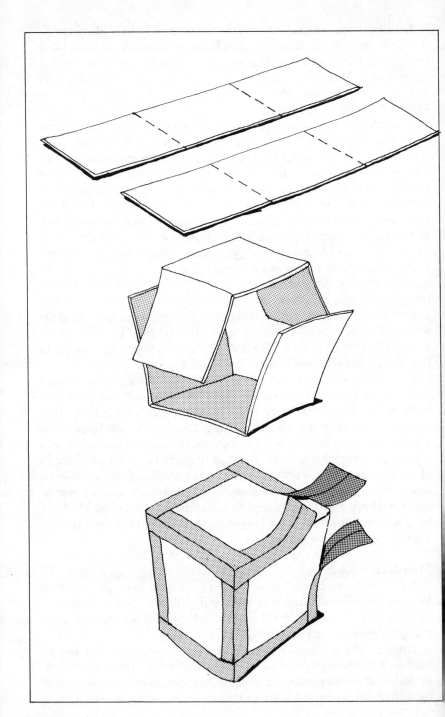

tration. Two of the folded strips should be put together as shown in the illustration and fastened together with strips of masking tape along all seams.

Once the blocks are constructed, kids can write words on them and decorate them. Each block could have six different words of the same kind and same part of speech, for example, one block could have all prepositions, such as under, behind, between, of, for and to. Another one might have all colors: red, green, black, blue, brown and yellow. Still another could use foods: spaghetti, ice cream, soup, toast, cookies, butter and hamburgers.

With a set of 10 or 15 blocks, a kid can come up with a vast number of word combinations. And added to the fun of making random word combinations can be the fun of literally building poems by stacking the blocks this way and that. Further, the blocks provide a wonderful way for kids to do word play with each other. Two or more kids can get their blocks together, multiplying the possibilities for word combinations, and build poem cities, sky-scrapers and castles. For younger kids in particular, word blocks really work to combine the fun of playing and building with blocks and the ever-new experiences of using words.

Word Badges

Here's an activity for getting kids to use the dictionary—they can learn brand-new and unusual words and learn to share them in a fun way. How is it done? By making word buttons or word badges they can pin onto their clothes.

To start this activity, provide the class with a number of dictionaries and ask each student to find an interesting word he didn't know before—maybe a long one (though longer words are more difficult to make into badges) or a funny-looking or funny-sounding one with x's or z's or q's, like "syzygy" or "quetzel." The kids, of course, should learn the definitions of their new word.

Once they've found their special words, the kids can make their word badges. One simple way to do this is to use adhesive-backed paper (the kind used for many convention-type name tags and for bumper stickers—check with a printer) and some political campaign or message-type pins ("Win with Whatsisname," "Have a Nice Day"—check a local campaign office or novelty store). Have the kids cut a circle out of the adhesive paper, using a diameter about a half-inch larger than the diameter of the message pin. With felt-tipped marking pens, have them write their word in the center of their cut-out circles. Then, along the circle's circumference, they should cut quarter-inch slits in toward the center (see the accom-

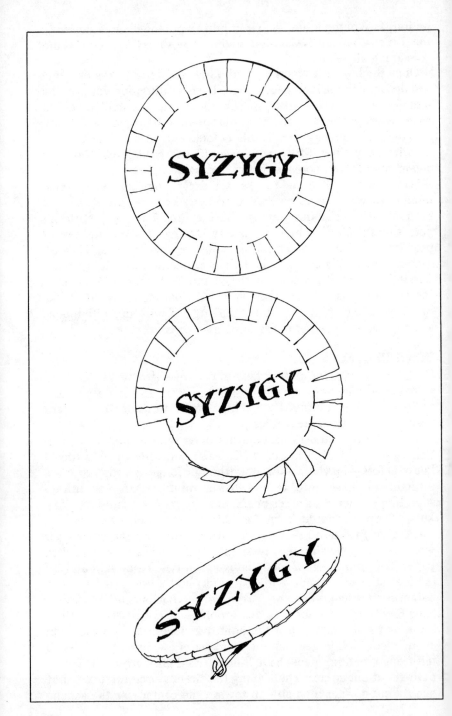

panying illustration), center the adhesive paper onto their pins, press the paper into place and fold the cut outer edges over the backs. Presto! Word badges!

Another word badge is simply a cardboard circle (corrugated board from old boxes or thick poster board will hold up well) with a safety pin taped to the back and the special word and a bright design drawn onto the front. Ambitious cutters might go baroque and make large badges by cutting entire words out of cardboard, decorating them with bright colors and taping a safety pin to the back.

Kids have a great time wearing word badges in class, around the school and at home. Few people will fail to ask them about their badges and they can have the fun of telling others about their special words. It's not unusual for some kids to get turned on by these badges and continue making them on their own, finding words that their classmates and even their teachers and parents don't know.

Poem Computers

Computers are doing a lot more today than adding and subtracting and guiding spaceships and keeping track of credit ratings. They're playing chess and writing music and yes, even making poems. Kids can build their own poem computers out of cardboard. Beginning with a short, simple poem, they can use their computers to come up with literally thousands of word combinations.

To make a poem computer, each child will need a 16- by 20-inch rectangle of cardboard, a 15- by 20-inch piece of poster board, a pair of scissors and six brass brads. To start, ask each child to cut six 1- by 3-inch holes in their cardboard rectangles, as shown in the drawing on page 30. Then ask them to cut 6-inch diameter circles from the poster board.

Next, have the class as a group write a six-word poem (not counting articles, and trying for several parts of speech)—maybe a simple nature poem:

> The owl hoots softly
> The full moon rises

or a crazy one:

> Sad bananas dance slowly
> In the cupboard

When the poem is constructed, have each kid, on her cardboard

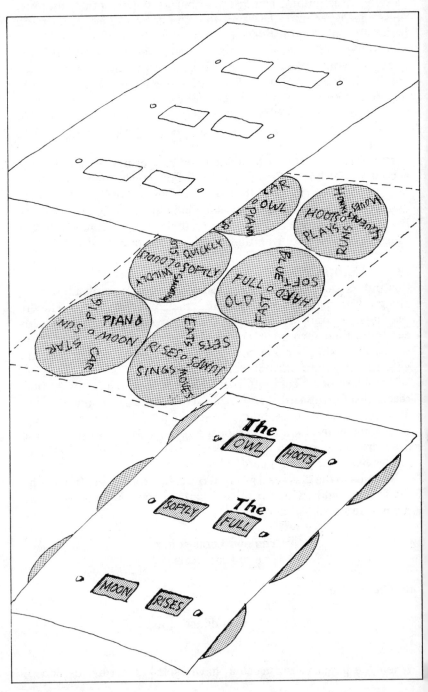

rectangle, write the articles in the poem above the appropriate 1- by 3-inch holes, as shown in the accompanying illustration. Then have them write one of the remaining words of the poem on each cut-out circle, as shown in the same illustration. Next, ask the kids to fill in each circle with other words of the same part of speech. There are no right words, none that are better than others. Kids should write any words that pop into their heads.

Once the circles are filled in, have the kids attach them to the cardboard rectangle with the brass brads, so that one word at a time will show through each slot. Have them set up the original poem first, then spin the discs at random, creating brand-new poems all the time. Poems children particularly like can be shared with the whole class, and the authors can write them down to keep.

Playing With Words

Language may be one of the most important growth and survival tools we have. With words we convey the information necessary to grow food, to build houses, to cure diseases. With words we transmit experiences and share ideas necessary for cooperative effort. Without any kind of language, each of us would be totally alone. Without our sophisticated verbal language, we would be much more at the mercy of the environment. Our language is the expression of our intellect, our problem-solving abilities. We are relatively puny beasts, neither swift nor strong enough to make much of a go of it with our physical attributes alone. Without language, we'd likely be extinct now. But our language isn't only a deadly serious business. It's a marvelous toy as well. Everybody plays with words, adults and children alike. Every crowd has its punsters, its crossword-puzzlers, its limerickers, its riddlers and double-acrostickers. We do love our words and our word games.

The activities in Chapter 2 are word games for kids to play in class. Some of the games are simply fun brain-stretchers; others relate more directly to the work of the poet. The first activity involves kids in making spontaneous (and usually nonsense) poems. The second and third activities deal with rhyme and rhythm, devices almost all poets use. The substituting games hook kids into poem and song making by having them substitute their own words for words in familiar poems and songs. The last activity works with kennings, literary devices less used now than in the past, but helpful in learning about how images, the heart of poetry, are made.

Word Choir

A word choir makes poems happen. The more kids in the choir, the more word combinations are possible. It may take some practice for the class to get really good at it, but once that happens, the choir can be an endless source of odd juxtapositions, crazy poems and much fun.

To make your word choir, you'll need a sentence like this one:

Spaghetti smiled green mustaches under bones.

The sentence has, and yours should have, nouns, a verb, an adjective and a preposition, so the choir will have four parts, corresponding to those parts of speech. When your sentence is ready, divide the class in half; tell the first half they will be nouns, and separate the remaining group into verbs, adjectives and prepositions. Once a child is assigned a part, he can pick his own word, or you can give him one. For the first few run-throughs, you should be the choir leader. Arrange the children in front of you and point to one kid at a time to say his word. It's likely to be pretty choppy and giggly at first, but after some practice things should smooth out (the giggles may never stop—that's a good sign!).

Once kids understand the game, they can take turns leading the choir. Each leader might make his own model sentence or poem and set the choir up himself, dividing the class into whatever parts of speech are in the sentence. Kids can also fiddle with variations. For instance, the word choir can build a long story instead of a brief nonsense sentence or crazy poem. There can be small groups for many parts of speech—including articles, adverbs, pronouns, conjunctions, etc. Instead of using only one word, each kid can change his word (as long as it's the same part of speech) every time the leader points to him. The choir also could incorporate sounds— swish, squeak, twang, flop—into its performances. (The made-up sounds in the fourth activity are good ones for the choir to use.) One sixth grade choir went on for a hilarious 20 minutes with only sounds, no words at all.

The class might like some of the word choir's creations so much that they'll want to save them. You could act as stenographer at word choir concerts, then ditto copies of the poems and stories for each student. Kids like to see and/or hear their own performances, too. If video tape or tape recording equipment is available, you might like to record some of the word choir masterpieces. The sixth grade group just mentioned liked their word choir so much they decided to perform for an Open House. Instead of giving a spontaneous performance, they chose their best creations, memorized them and spoke them in unison as choral readings.

Rhyming Games

A poem is actually a tuneless song; it makes its own music with cadences and the sounds of words. Rhyme is a music-making device. Though it's not widely used by modern poets, it is still a part of poetry. Playing with rhymes is a good way to explore how poetry makes music with words.

One way to play with rhymes is to have the class divide into pairs. (They can choose their own partners or you can do the pairing.) Have one child in each pair say a word—for example, "sand" —and ask the other child to respond with a rhyming word— "hand." After a few minutes, have the kids switch—the one who was the initiator becomes the responder, the one who first responded now initiates. Soon enough, the pairs will run out of Dr. Seuss rhymes or will become bored with predictable rhymes— June/moon, hat/cat, bed/red. This will give you the opportunity to talk about rhymes: that the best ones, the really fun ones, are almost always surprises; that rhyming June with prune is a lot more interesting than rhyming June with moon.

As the pairs continue to play with words, try to encourage them to find ever more unusual rhymes. You can also introduce them to half-rhymes—words that have a similar sound but don't really rhyme, such as cup/cap, boat/bone, moon/mean, bed/bad, roof/ truth, light/late, clock/cloak—as a way of coming up with many more appealing musical word combinations.

After a few periods of playing with simple rhyming words, pairs of kids can begin to make rhyming (or half-rhyming) couplets. The format is the same—have one child initiate, the other child respond: I ate some cheese/and fell on my knees; I took a nap/wearing my baseball cap; I pulled some weeds/they made me sneeze; I climbed to the roof/and drank some orange juice; we played in the park/because we didn't have to work. Encourage your kids to be as imaginative, unusual, silly and crazy as they can be when making their couplets. Tell them that for now, rhythms and correct cadences don't matter. Later, rhyming and rhythms can be used together (see the following activity). If some kids get tired of saying their couplets to each other, they might like to write down the ones they think are good and share them with the whole class.

Rhythm Games

While rhyme is less in favor in modern poetry than it was in the poetry of the past, rhythm remains absolutely central. Today we do not look for rhythms of the sonnet or the heroic couplet, in which every line has the same cadence, but the various rhythms of phrases within a poem.

Before kids start mixing cadences in free-verse poems, they ought to develop a sense of rhythms. Simply put, rhythms are combinations of accented and unaccented sounds. Kids can begin to play with them without words at all—using hand claps or sounds like "dah." When you begin, try to work with the class as a whole, leading kids in rhythmic chants or clapping. Start with the basic meters—iambic, trochaic, anapestic, dactylic, spondaic. The *iamb* is an unaccented sound followed by an accented one—dah DAH. The whole class together can chant dah DAH dah DAH dah DAH dah DAH dah DAH (five iambs together make the old familiar iambic pentameter), perhaps punctuating the accented DAHs with claps or foot stamps (depending on your willingness to rattle the roof). The *trochaic* meter reverses the iambic—DAH dah DAH dah DAH dah DAH dah DAH dah. *Anapestic* goes like this: dah dah DAH dah dah DAH dah dah DAH dah dah DAH dah dah DAH (two unaccented syllables followed by one accented syllable). And the *dactylic* meter reverses that: DAH dah dah DAH dah dah DAH dah dah DAH dah dah DAH dah dah. *Spondaic* meter is composed of two equally accented sounds together: DAH DAH.

When you start, have the class spend a period or two chanting the various basic rhythms. Then, have them start combining rhythms:

> dah DAH dah DAH
> dah dah DAH dah dah DAH

or

> dah DAH dah dah DAH dah dah DAH
> DAH dah DAH dah DAH dah
> DAH DAH DAH DAH
> DAH dah dah DAH dah dah DAH dah

Once the kids are familiar with the different rhythms, they can start using words instead of "dahs." Provide the kids with some models for each kind of meter: iambic—unTIL, good-BYE, reTURN, aBOUT; trochaic—TURKey, PURple, BARber, MUScle; anapestic—underSTAND, introDUCE, recomMEND, HalloWEEN; dactylic—ELephant, HAPpiness, LAUNdromat, COLoring; spondaic—MOONLIGHT, DAYBREAK, BRAINSTORM. Kids can find other words to fit each kind of meter. If they get tired of chanting they can make up rhythm sentences and write them down.

Next, have the class work with metered lines, using more than one word. For instance, iambic pentameter:

> dah DAH dah DAH dah DAH dah DAH dah DAH
> I ate my breakfast then I went to school

or dactylic trimeter:

> DAH dah dah DAH dah dah DAH dah dah
> Practicing dancing with buffalo

or combinations:

> dah DAH dah dah DAH
> dah DAH dah DAH
> dah DAH dah dah DAH
> dah DAH
>
> my hat blew away
> my hair stood up
> I ran to my house
> and sneezed

Once they get used to fitting words and rhythms together, kids can try using rhyming words. The fun and familiar limerick form is a good one to start with:

> dah DAH dah dah DAH dah dah DAH
> dah DAH dah dah DAH dah dah DAH
> dah DAH dah dah DAH dah
> dah DAH dah dah DAH dah
> dah DAH dah dah DAH dah dah DAH

When they put in words, tell the children to rhyme the first, second and fifth lines, and the third and fourth lines:

> A gentle young daughter named Sue
> Decided at last what to do.
> Her Mom screamed and bellowed,
> Her Dad snarled and yelled, so
> She found them a home in the zoo.

Eventually your students may invent rhythm and rhyme forms of their own.

Onomatopoeia and Other Noises

Kids seem to love onomatopoetic words, ones that "sound like they mean"—the "buzz" of a bee, the "whoosh" of a gust of wind, the "splash" of water, the "tick-tock" of a clock. Kids can start playing with onomatopoeia by identifying the onomatopoetic words we already have as part of our language—crack, click, zip, bang, thump, swoop, gurgle, clip-clop, wheeze, swish, chuckle, hiss, chortle, quack and so on. They can write stories using as many of these words as possible, then read the stories for the whole class, exaggerating and dramatizing the sounds. A variation of such story and song writing involves one or more members of the class repeating "sound effect" words in appropriate places:

> The man laughed "chuckle chuckle"
>
> The gun went off "bang bang"
>
> The woman dived into the water "splash"

The best fun comes when the kids have a good sense of these sound-words and start making up their own. The most lively creations often occur when children invent sounds for unusual, unlikely things: What sound does a carrot make? a pineapple? a banana? spinach? an egg? peanut butter? What sound does a chair make? a stone? a rug? a shovel? a rope? a lamp? Ask your kids to invent the sounds, then figure out how to spell them. If they're interested, they can stage mini-dramas in which inanimate characters utter their invented sounds.

Guessing games with new sound-words can be fun, too. Have each student make a list of five or more objects, then invent a sound for each. One at a time, ask each child to write his or her list of objects on the chalk board, then pronounce each sound as the class tries to match the sound with the object. Another guessing game involves creating sounds for elaborate situations:

> What is the sound of starlight striking a stone?
> * t * a * h *
>
> What is the sound of someone chewing a piece of eggshell?
> cchkkt!

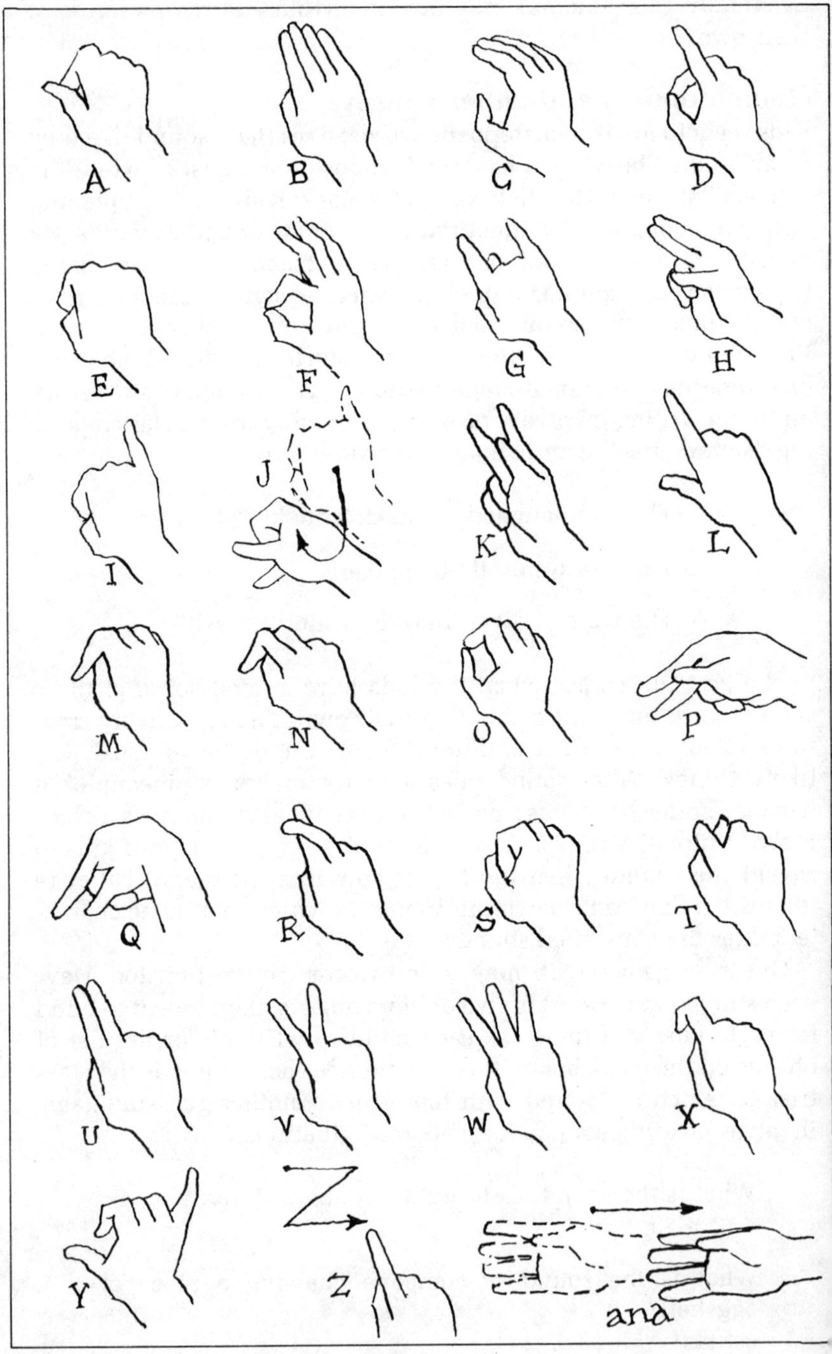

A B C D

E F G H

I J K L

M N O P

Q R S T

U V W X

Y Z ana

> What is the sound of a foot wearing a tennis shoe stepping on a rotten tomato?
> ssheeushsh

You can provide the situations to begin with, or give the kids a few models and let them have at it themselves. The more extreme and fantastic the situations, the more fun there will be.

Sign Language

Kids are fascinated by words-without-sounds—sign language. Learning sign language isn't only fun for kids, it's another dimension of language experience; it helps them to understand that language as they use it isn't an absolute, that it isn't defined narrowly by vocal utterances. Instead it is defined broadly as a set of symbols, vocal or otherwise, that conveys information.

If your class is interested, help them to learn the mute alphabet, shown on page 38. If possible, provide each student with his own copy of this alphabet of gestures—learning it can grow tedious, so it's best to practice only two or three letters each time, rather than devoting entire periods to sign language, and let those kids who wish to study it on their own time. Once kids have mastered it, they'll likely enjoy conversing with each other by spelling out words with their hands.

But sign language is more than just hand spelling. Kids will catch on quickly that that's a relatively slow and clumsy process. The next step is to develop gestures for whole words and phrases—your students can create their own manual vocabularies. First, have the class identify a certain number of words and phrases they want to develop signs for; try to encourage a good mix of parts of speech. Then, working together as a group, have them create their signs. Remind them from time to time to keep the signs simple and direct and as "readable" as possible—you might suggest pointing to the heart for "love," pointing to the head for "think," two fingers in walking motion for "walk," one palm resting on another for "on," arms spread wide apart for "big" and similar familiar gestures. Kids will probably find that they won't be able to develop simple signs for all the words they want to use, so they may have to combine spelling signs with whole-word ones.

Eventually, most of your class should be able to carry on rather long conversations with each other using sign language, and a few class periods could be given over entirely to conversing with gestures. As a special project, some kids might try presenting stories and poems in sign language. Others might develop picture languages, or they might study such code languages as semaphore and Morse code.

Special Languages

In all those World War II movies, the American soldiers always discover the enemy infiltrator in one of two ways: asking him a question about American sports, such as who made the last out in the '38 World Series, or speaking to him in Pig Latin and expecting a reply. Both are things every true-blue, red-blooded American knows about. The World Series may not have a place in many curriculums, but Pig Latin and other special or silly languages can fit nicely into language/writing/word play activities.

It shouldn't take long for students to pick up the basics of Pig Latin. Tell them that the way to speak it is to lift the initial sound from a word and tack it on to the end of the word, and follow that sound with a long "A" sound—"ay." "Pig" becomes "ig-pay"; "latin" changes to "atin-lay." (Pig Latin scholars differ on the correct way to deal with initial vowel sounds. Some prefer the more formal Roman Mode, pronouncing the word as is and adding an "ay" at the end—apple-ay—rather than the more modern Constantinople Variation, which suggests pronouncing the word only—apple.) It will help the kids if you write lots of Pig Latin examples on the board and then pronounce the words for them. Have the class practice their Pig Latin in a couple of class periods, and it's likely they'll continue to practice at recess, after school and at home as well.

Once the kids have mastered the language, you can hold a whole-class discussion in Pig Latin. You can also sing familiar songs in Pig Latin—can you guess this one?

> ow-ray, ow-ray, ow-ray our-yay oat-bay
> ently-gay own-day e-thay eam-stray
> errily-may, errily-may, errily-may, errily-may
> ife-lay is-ay ut-bay a-ay eam-dray

Singing like this can get pretty hilarious and the class may not make it through a whole song, but the kids will certainly love it.

Another special language has its roots in traveling carnivals. "Carny" was spoken, so the story goes, by people working in carnivals so that the "rubes" couldn't understand them. Carny is somewhat more complicated than Pig Latin, but just as much fun to speak. It's spoken by adding an extra syllable to every syllable of the word one is saying—the author uses "izz" for the extra syllable, the kids on the TV show "Zoom" use "ib," or you can make up your own. The extra syllable comes right after the initial sound of each syllable—Carny becomes C-izz-arn-izz-y; book is b-izz-ook; teacher is t-izz-each-izz-er; banana is b-izz-an-izz-an-izz-a. If a word begins with a vowel sound, put the extra syllable in front—apple becomes izz-app-izz-le, orange becomes izz-or-izz-ange. You'll probably need to devote more time to Carny than to Pig Latin. Even after the kids learn to speak it, they'll find they have a tough time understanding it when someone else speaks it.

Besides learning these special languages, your kids might like to make up languages of their own. For a whole-class project, ask your students to identify a certain number of words they use often, then agree on a brand-new made-up word to substitute for each and record the new words in a Class Language Dictionary. This kind of project works best if it's done in little bits over a period of several weeks. It gives kids a chance to build their language slowly, rather than having to memorize it all at once. Once they've accumulated a fairly large vocabulary, have the class spend one period in which only the new language is spoken (they'll probably need to mix in a few regular English words for which they didn't create equivalents).

If your students enjoy playing with special languages, you might consider introducing them to Esperanto, the international language. You can find out more about this language by reading *Esperanto* and the *Esperanto Pocket Dictionary* (see the resource list).

Hink Pinks, Teakettles and Ghosts

Here are three word games that kids have been playing for a long time. They're lots of fun but they also demand some thought about and work with words.

"Hink Pinks" are riddles that have two-word rhyming answers:

> What does a rodent wear on its head?
> A rat hat.
>
> What do you call a male deer trapped in quicksand?
> A stuck buck.
>
> What do you call a light-colored garden pest?
> A pale snail.

"Hinky Pinkies" are riddles that need rhyming answers with two syllables:

What do you call a really good film?
A groovy movie.

What do you call it when cows fight?
A cattle battle.

What do you call it when the joke is over?
After laughter.

"Hinkety Pinketies" are riddles that have rhyming answers with three syllables:

What do you do when you think about last Christmas?
Remember December.

What will it take to clean up the air?
Pollution solution.

What do you call a melon that a swift, long-horned mammal eats?
Antelope cantaloupe.

Your class can learn to make hink pinks and their variations by first thinking of a rhyming answer, then making up an appropriate question. A dictionary of rhyming words can be a great help. (One such dictionary, Rhyming Dictionary, is published by Barnes and Noble.) Kids can also use regular dictionaries and thesauri to help them write the questions so they don't give the answer away (e.g., saying "swift, long-horned mammal" instead of "antelope"). You can devote part of a class to making up the riddles, the rest to sharing them with the whole class.

Puns have a bad reputation, but to some they are irresistible, even in the wake of the terrible groaning that is certain to follow. (Maybe we need a Pun Liberation Movement to get puns out of the closets and into the mainstream of wit, where they belong.) "Teakettle" is a pun game. The object is to make up a sentence in which a double-meaning word occurs twice, once having one meaning, once having the other. Then you present the sentence with the word left out—in its place you use the word "teakettle":

After the man paid for all the dishes he "teakettle,"
he was completely "teakettle."

The missing word is "broke." Here are some more examples:

After the "teakettle" finished the baseball game,
he drank a whole "teakettle" of lemonade.
(pitcher)

Before the house painter put on another "teakettle,"
he decided to take off his "teakettle."
(coat)

They took the shortest "teakettle" to the stadium
so they'd be on time to "teakettle" for the home
team.
(route/root—This kind of pun is called a homo-
phone. It uses words that sound alike but have
different spellings. Homonym puns use words that
are spelled alike and sound alike.)

Right after the wedding the "teakettle" had to
"teakettle" his favorite horse.
(groom)

"Ghost" is a vocabulary and spelling game for older kids. One
person begins by saying a letter, "b," for example. The second
person adds a letter, perhaps "i." The third player adds a letter to
these two. If she adds a letter that completes the spelling of a word,
the round is over and a new one begins. When a player adds a
letter, it must be one that she knows can lead to the spelling of a
real word. A player can't, for example, add an "x" to a "b." If the
following player wishes, she can challenge the one who's just
added a letter, who must say the word he had in mind to prove that
the addition is correct; if he can't prove it, the round ends.

If scoring is important to your students, assign a player one letter
from the word "ghost" each time he loses or adds an incorrect
letter—"g" for the first loss, "h" for the second and so on—until
he's lost five rounds—g-h-o-s-t—and the game is over. If your class
would rather keep the game noncompetitive, they can play "Infin-
ity Ghost," in which the whole class together tries to build the
longest words possible.

New Words in Old Songs and Poems
This activity is a back door into poem making. You start by changing a single word in a familiar song or poem, then work backwards
and forwards from it until you've got a whole new song or poem.

"Row, row, row your boat" is a good song to work with. The

following is one way you and your class might end up changing the song's lyrics:

A boat's a kind of vehicle. What other kinds of vehicles are there?

A car, a bus, an airplane.

Let's take a car. Row, row, row your car . . . .
You don't row a car; what do you do?

Drive.

So let's change "row" to "drive."
Drive, drive, drive your car
Gently down the stream . . . .
Would you rather have the car driving somewhere else?

Road, street.

OK. Drive, drive, drive your car
Gently, down the street . . . .
How about "gently"? Do you want to drive that way?

Slowly.

Drive, drive, drive your car
Slowly down the street
Merrily, merrily, merrily, merrily . . . .

Do you want to keep merrily? What about a car noise?

Rrhum-rrhum, beep-beep, honk.

Drive, drive, drive your car
Slowly down the street
Honk honk beep beep
Life is . . . What?

Life is really neat. Life is such a treat.

Drive, drive, drive your car
Slowly down the street

Honk honk beep beep
Life is such a treat

No Pulitzer Prize here, true. But a brand-new song has been built out of an old one. Working this way, inside-out really, is very effective in helping kids relate to cadences without ever discussing an abstract concept of meter at all. When your students are substituting words and phrases, they have to match the rhythms of the poem or song they're working with. Very often, kids demonstrate an unspoken sense of correct meter and supply appropriate words. If they don't, you can make a simple comparison of words or lines to illuminate the issue:

> Fly fly fly your airplane. . . .
> doesn't quite fit with
> Row row row your boat. . . .
> try
> Fly fly fly your plane

When you first begin to substitute new words for old, have the whole class do two or three songs together; then let the kids try working out new lyrics individually. One fourth grade boy worked long and zealously at re-doing "Home on the Range":

> Oh give me a town
> Where the children don't frown
> Where the girls and the boys always play
> The kids all play ball
> And there's no school at all
> 'Cause the teachers have all gone away

There's no reason to stick with childhood songs and nursery rhymes. Older kids often like to do this activity with their favorite popular songs. A few years ago some seventh graders turned the Beatles' "Rocky Raccoon" into "Jerry Giraffe" and got lots of laughs. There's also no need to stick with strictly metered and rhymed forms, but kids do seem to like those the best. One favorite is Blake's "Tyger, tyger, burning bright," which has become everything from "Ice cream, ice cream, melting fast" to "Chicken, chicken, squawking loud."

C D B
William Steig has written and illustrated an absolutely delightful

book called *C D B!* On the cover is a drawing of a boy pointing to a bee about to land on a flower. The boy exclaims, "C D B!" And so the book goes, with sentences concocted of "words" that are single letters or single numbers. It's wonderfully funny stuff.

Kids not only love the book, they love to make up their own sentences and stories using single letters and numbers. When you start, have them look at Steig's book first (see the resource list) or the models given below. Show them how letter sounds often can stand for or sound like whole words. You might want to provide them with a few sentences or stories to begin with, then let them loose on their own. Drawings accompanying the "sentences" help kids to get the point.

D N-M-L S A B-U-T

Y S E 1-N O-A?

I F A M-R

I 8 D C-T
D C-T S 2 B-Z

R U O-L?
S I M

D E-L S N D C

Ladle By Brew

At a poetry workshop a while ago, there was a retelling of the story of Hansel and Gretel. The title of the new version indicates what this "genre" is all about: "Edsel ant Griddle." The point is to substitute for each word in a story a word that sounds almost like it—Hansel, Edsel; Gretel, Griddle. The new version will sound strangely and hilariously like a fractured sound track from a foreign film.

When kids play this word game in the classroom, it never fails to produce abundant laughter. But there's more to the game than fun—the activity is an excellent vocabulary builder, since to make it work, kids will need to consult the dictionary constantly. (It's not very easy to write these stories; younger kids may have a difficult time.) Proper nouns are OK, but no homonyms or foreign words should be used (it'll sound properly foreign without them). Here are some examples kids can use as models:

Little Boy Blue
Come blow your horn
The sheep's in the meadow
The cow's in the corn
Where is the boy
Who looks after the sheep?
He's under the haystack
Fast asleep

Ladle By Brew
Cub low year hoard
There sleeps under mellow
Thick housing acorn
Why razz thereby
Woo locks aster thresh heap?
His wonder there ace tack
Fist is leap

Once upon a time there was a hare who bragged to everyone about how fast he could run. He challenged all the animals to race and he never lost. A tortoise, who was tired of the hare's boasting, said, "I could beat you in a race." The hare laughed and laughed. But the tortoise said again, "I could beat you in a race." This made the hare angry, so he challenged the tortoise to race.

The race began and in a flash the hare was out of sight, and the tortoise just walked slowly along. The hare looked back and could not see the tortoise anywhere, so he decided to take a rest before finishing the race. He slept under a big tree. After a while the tortoise caught up with the hare, who was still sleeping, and tiptoed quietly past him and kept on his way. Later the hare woke up and ran to the finish line. But the tortoise, who had just walked steadily on, was already there.

Ones ponder dime throw us say here hub ragged tow waver rayon hub out oar aster cud drone. Each Al lynched owl they are nibbles tore ace, Andy neighbor loft. Ate oar toss, hoe worrse tar dove there hears bow sting, sad, "Ah cud be chewing erase." There here left Dan left. Butter tore toss sad akin, "Ah cud chewing erase." Dismayed there here Ann grease oh each Al lynched there tore toss tore ace.

There ace big Ann end dinner flesh there here whiz ah
tough side, end there tore toss chess squawked slur lee
ale lung. There here locked beck end cud nazi tore toss
in knee wear, sue heed ease sigh dead tote ache arrest
biff orphan itching there ace. Ease leapt endear rub bag
tray. Of tarot isle there tore toss caw top wither here hoe
worse steel slay ping, end dipped oat choired lee bass
Tim end cap Don ease sway. Lay tar there here woe cup
end wren toe there fin itch lion, butter tore toss hoe head
chess squawked stud deal lawn, Warsaw reedy dare.

After they've reworded a few of their favorite poems or stories,
some kids may want to perform them as "dramatic" readings, or
delightful narratives for pantomime skits.

Nonsense Poems

After your kids have experimented with rhythms and have made
some rhythm forms to fit words into, they can use the same forms
for their own, homemade nonsense word poems. Tell them they
can use any words, real or not, to fit to the meter of the poem you or
they work out—often, kids like to combine real words with ones
they make up, and even include words they know from other languages. In this activity, the sound's the thing; it's poetic anarchy.

Here's an example of a nonsense poem using iambic meter:

> dah DAH dah DAH dah DAH dah DAH
> dah DAH dah DAH dah DAH
> dah DAH dah DAH dah DAH dah DAH
> dah DAh dah DAH dah DAH
>
> The grummer ur the pavel blanz
> A dog's poliff for booch
> Wex arkint zam li quanter yang
> Dus shindog meezy vooch

After they make up a few, some of your kids may want to perform
their nonsense poems for the whole class.

Kennings

A kenning is a special kind of metaphor that was common in
Anglo-Saxon and early Germanic poetry—it's a compound noun
used in place of a single noun. Though they're not much used
today, kennings can give kids a real sense of what metaphor is all

about. Making up kennings can show your students that many different words can enable them to speak and write about the world.

In kennings, neither word in the compound noun is the real name of the thing being talked about ("whale road" for "ocean"). Some of the Anglo-Saxon kennings may be familiar to you if you've taken an English literature course or two: swan path—sky; sword water—blood; battle wolf—warrior. But when you start working with kennings, you'll probably want to provide your class with models that are more familiar to them than warriors and mead halls. Here are a few:

> car—wheel beast
> sleep—dream cave
> TV—picture box
> sky—star garden
> school—learning house
> stove—fire box
> moon—light ball

After you discuss the make-up of the kenning and show your class several examples, let the students make kennings on their own. (This is a good activity to do in small groups.) When groups have produced a few brand-new kennings, they can present them to the entire class and see who can tell what they mean.

Spoonerisms

The Reverend William A. Spooner was a British clergyman who suffered from the unfortunate propensity for mixing up the sounds of words when he spoke. A bowl of soup was likely to become a "sowl of boup" when Reverend Spooner said it; the House of Lords might have left his lips as the "Louse of Hords"; and smoking a pipe could have turned into "poking a smipe." So famous did his bloopers become that Spooner's name became a part of the language: "spoonerism, n. a transposition of (usually) initial sounds of two or more words that generally creates a comic effect."

Most kids seem to delight in spoonerisms in casual word play. They can have the same fun by writing a whole story filled with spoonerisms. To begin, provide your kids with a model such as the one that follows. Give each student a copy of the story's standard version and a copy of the spoonerized version; then read them both aloud and ask the kids to follow along, allowing for lots of giggling on the second version. After that, the whole class can choose a

light ball

star garden

wheel beast

familiar story to spoonerize, and work on it as a group. Finally, each student can work on his or her own masterpiece.

"The Three Billy Goats Gruff"

Once upon a time there were three billy goats who lived in a pasture. There was a stream next to their pasture and another pasture on the other side, with a bridge in between. Underneath the bridge lived a mean troll. One day the three billy goats decided to cross the bridge and graze on the fresh grass on the other side. The littlest billy goat went first. When the troll heard him he said, "Who's on my bridge?" The billy goat answered, "It is I, a little billy goat." "I'm going to eat you," said the troll. "Oh, please don't!" said the little billy goat. "My brother is larger and will make a better meal." So the troll decided to wait and he let the billy goat go. Then the next billy goat walked across the bridge. "Who's on my bridge?" said the troll. "It is I, a middle-sized billy goat," said the middle-sized billy goat. "I'm going to eat you," said the troll. "Oh, please don't," said the middle-sized billy goat. "My brother is larger and will make a better meal." So the troll decided to wait and he let the billy goat go. Then the next billy goat walked across the bridge. "Who's on my bridge?" said the troll. "It is I, a big billy goat." "I'm going to eat you," said the troll. "Come and try it," said the big billy goat. And when the troll came up to eat him, the big strong billy goat knocked him off the bridge and he was never seen again.

"The Gree Thrilly Boats Guff"

Once uton a pime there were gee thrilly boats who pived in a lasture. There was a stream past to their nexture and apother nasture on the other side, brith a widge in between. Underbreath the nidge lived a trean moll. One day the gee thrilly boats decided to boss the cridge and graze on the gresh fass on the other side. The bittlest gilly loat fent wirst. Tren the wholl heard him he said, "Bro's on my whidge?" The gilly boat answered, "It is I, a gittle lilly boat." "I'm going to eat you," traid the soll. "Oh, dease plon't!" laid the sittle gilly boat. "My lother is brager and will bake a metter meal." Tro the soll wecided to date and get the gilly boat lo. Then the next gilly boat bralked across the widge. "Bro's on my whidge?" traid the soll. "It is I, a siddle-mized gilly boat." "I'm going to eat you," traid the soll. "Oh, dease plon't!" said the siddle-mized gilly boat. "My lother is brager and will bake a metter meal." Tro the soll wecided to date and get the gilly boat lo. Then the next gilly boat bralked across the widge. "Bro's on my whidge?" traid the soll. "It is I, a big gilly boat." "I'm going to eat you," traid the soll. "Trome and cy it!" baid the sig gilly boat. And tren the wholl came eap to ut the gilly boat, the strig bong gilly boat brocked him off the knidge and he was sever neen again.

Names for Stores

The merchant and the poet generally don't hang out together, but there's always room in the world of commerce for a bit of imaginative wording. Take store names, for instance. Is there any reason a fabric store should be called Jones Yardage when it could be called Sew and Sew instead? What about changing Ralph the Florist into Good and Planty? Wouldn't anyone like to go to a pastry shop called Just Desserts, or an optometrist's named The Eyes Have It? How about a furniture store called Sitting Pretty, a sporting goods store called Have a Ball, a cobbler's shop called Taming of the Shoe, a donut shop called The Hole Thing?

To get kids going on this creative name activity, provide your class with a few models, then ask them to make up a few more store names as a group. When they're familiar with the idea, have the kids divide into small groups and continue the activity. The store names don't have to be phrases with puns in them—they can also be descriptive or picturesque names like Sizzler Steak Houses, Wheeler Dealer Bike Shops, Trees Please Nurseries or Word World Bookstores.

PART TWO

Introduction

What is this thing called "poem"? There are countless essays and books on poetics and aesthetics that worry endlessly over that very question—and they come to no clear or absolute definitions. Ultimately, everyone will get more of an understanding of what poetry is from his or her own experiences with poems than from an infinite collection of learned declarative sentences. It's more important to develop a "sense" of poetry than a definition. That's why reading poetry is so very important for anyone who wants to write it. Reading poetry deepens that sense of what poetry is, of what it's all about. For every minute spent discussing what a poem is, kids ought to spend an hour reading poems and writing them.

Still, the question is real and present: What is a poem? And though the teacher ought not to spend too much time lecturing, her students can gain some insight from a kind of general definition.

A poem is a more-or-less compact expression of a poet's response to the world. When you touch a hot stove, you pull your hand away and say, "Ouch!" A poem is like that "Ouch!" It doesn't need to be a story of what happened (though poems can tell stories, too)—you don't say, "I just put my hand on the hot stove and I pulled it away and it really, really hurt." You just say, "Ouch!" Most of our experiences are more complicated than putting a hand on the stove. Most of our responses are complex interminglings of an inner and an outer world, so most poems are more complicated than just "Ouch!" At the very center, though, poems are responses, just like "Ouch" and "Wow" and "Far out."

But people don't write poems in order to experience the world— they write poems to express their experiences to somebody else, to

55

somehow share them. So a poem has to have information: why, where, what and so on. It has to provide a way for somebody else to get a sense of a poet's experience, to feel in some way what the poet felt. That's what a poem is "about," that sharing of experience; that's what a poem "means." (No matter how tempted you may become, however, try not to ask students what a poem means. Ask instead, "What do you feel when you read this poem? Happy? Sad? Confused?" It may not be the perfect question—if there is one—but it keeps the poem pumping and breathing, and keeps it from being a dead object instead of a live experience. One more thing—try not to answer the question yourself—if you do, your answer may become the "right" answer, and that, of course, can stop all discussion.)

The following two chapters deal directly with the process of making poems, with nurturing specific skills the poet works with and with specific poetic devices and forms. The chapters include some "starters"—ideas for poems, kinds of poems—but the emphasis isn't on gimmicks. As Phillip Lopate said in his book *Being With Children,* "Pound did not write 'The Cantos' by looking at an ambiguous photograph, nor did Rilke [write] 'The Duino Elegies' by starting each line with a color." Too many gimmicks can prevent beginning writers from doing the real work necessary to develop poetic skills; they can prevent them from confronting their own raw experiences, finding the poetry in them and taking the risks of turning them into words for others to read.

Several of the activities in Part II encourage kids to read and respond to each other's poems. As we said earlier, it is as important to read poems as it is to discuss and write them, so part of every writing period should be given to sharing the poems your kids have written. (Some kids, however, may be shy about sharing their work, so don't force anyone who doesn't want to join in.) This action will round out the poetic process—from the raw experiences of one person, through his personal responses and interpretations, onto the page and out to an audience. Every poet, from beginner to master, needs the chance to share what he's done.

Using the Poet's Tools

This chapter pays particular attention to the tools poets work with, to the skills and techniques necessary for making and understanding poetry and to the "sensibility" that gives birth to poems.

Poetic techniques involve the ability to handle words. This means using rhyme, imagery, alliteration and rhythm to achieve desired effects. In the first two chapters of this book, there were activities that dealt with rhyme, alliteration and rhythm. In Chapter 3 there are activities on building images using similes and metaphors, on quickening language by turning nouns into verbs, on understanding and experimenting with poetic lines.

Besides technique, the poet cultivates a sensibility, a way of seeing and responding to the world. Several of the activities in Chapter 3 are intended to help kids develop abilities to deepen this poetic sensibility. Journal keeping, observation, stream-of-consciousness writing and "finding" poems all do more than simply teach technique—they require young writers to enlarge their perspectives and grow their consciousness so that poetry can fit in.

Journals

All young writers should have their own journals, not necessarily to write poems in but to record impressions, feelings, thoughts, experiences, ideas for poems, images, interesting words. Journals can be loose-leaf binders or spiral notebooks for kids to use as they will—they can decorate them and draw pictures on them as well as write in them. (Some kids may want to make up fancy pen names for themselves to use on the covers of their journals and on their poems.) The journals can be used for many of the activities in this chapter.

Once your kids are comfortable using their journals, you can encourage them to include other things in them besides classroom activities. Tell them they can record whatever seems to be pertinent to their writing. Also tell them that their journals are not simply diaries, but tools for exploring themselves and their writing and places to keep things that may become poems or parts of poems. When they have interesting ideas or new experiences, they can write about them in their journals. When they're feeling strong emotions, they can explain and explore them in their journals. When they read poems they especially like, they can copy them into their journals. When they find new words that appeal to them, they can list them in their journals.

After a few classes using the journal for specific activities, you'll probably want to set aside regular journal-writing times, parts of writing periods or an occasional full writing period for the kids to write in their journals on their own. Since journals may contain much personal writing as well as assigned activities, be careful to respect kids' privacy and read them only with their permission.

Lines

"How come poetry is always written in those funny lines, instead of like stories?" Kids are particularly inclined to ask this question, and no answer seems wholly satisfactory—the less we know about poetry and its roots in music, the more those line breaks may be confusing to us. Without getting deeply involved in an abstruse discussion of poetics, it can be said that the often strange-seeming line breaks are used to indicate the rhythms of the poem. (See Chapter 2 for work with rhythms.) They are a kind of punctuation that indicates a pause or the end of a rhythmic unit.

This explanation is fine as far as it goes, but, like too many explanations, it doesn't go very far toward developing a real understanding. To learn more about line breaks, it's necessary to get a feel for them, to experiment with them and see how they actually work in poems.

One way to do this is to present each of your students with a copy of a poem rewritten in prose style, and have the kids break it into lines of poetry. Each student, if he wants to, can then read his or her version to the class. After everyone in the class has had the chance to read, distribute copies of the poem as it was originally written and hold a class discussion on the how's and why's of the line breaks the poet used.

Another way to study poetic lines is for kids to use their own poems and write several versions of them, breaking lines differently each time. The student poet can read her own various versions aloud to the class, or better, with permission, you or another student can read them. After each poem has been read in its different manifestations, the class can discuss the relative merits of each variation. This may not be the way to arrive at a carefully worded explanation of the reason for line breaks, but it can help kids internalize a sense of how poetic lines function, and give them a sense of the sounds and rhythms that operate in poetry.

Observation

In poetry, no philosophical statement, no matter how profound, startling or well-worded, can have the same impact as just the right specific detail. And impact is what poetry is all about, whether it is the impact of recognition and affirmation—"Yes! That's so. I know it's true. It's the same as my own experience"—or the impact of discovery—"I'd never known that (felt that) before."

To create maximum impact, the really good poem hooks into specific, concrete details that the reader can see, hear, smell, taste, touch. Since the senses are the doors to emotions and thoughts, it is through the senses that a poem works on its readers. The poet, therefore, must have an eye for details, for the concrete facts of the outer world; he must also be able to use those details freely and gracefully in his poems. In learning to write poetry, kids need to cultivate their abilities as observers.

The personal journals discussed earlier can be used for this activity. You can begin by asking the students to write down in their journals everything they can see, hear, taste, touch and smell in the classroom in a given period of time—say 10 or 15 minutes. Tell them they are free to move around, to touch things, lift things, explore surfaces, textures, contours. They can smell things they don't normally relate to by smelling—chalk, paper, scissors, erasers. They can listen to the sounds of cloth rustling, pencils writing on paper, desks scraping on the floor, books being opened and closed. As they record their observations, they can make them as simple or as complicated as they wish. And they don't have to write whole sentences:

> squeaking door
> pencil scratching on paper
> teacher moving from desk to desk
> Nancy smiling at Ann
> Tom's untied shoe
> my hands smell like soap

> bookcase is broken
> clock makes a buzzing sound
> chalk is smooth and dusty
> banging in the hall
> book cover feels cold
> black mark on the floor

At the end of the 10- or 15-minute period, ask the kids to stop writing and read their lists to the whole class. This will give everybody a chance to see what the others observed, what they might have missed themselves or something they were the only one to notice.

After the kids have done this activity in the classroom, they can do it somewhere else—in the library or the gym, on the playground or on a walk around the block. When they've done their observations once or twice with journals in hand, they can try observing without pencil and paper, then record later as many of their observations as they can remember. In every case, it's important that the whole class meet after the activity, so that the kids can share their observations with each other.

Another observation activity involves a single object. In the classroom it can be something like a desk, a globe, a slide projector, even a person. You can place the object in front of the class and ask each student to write as many observations about it as he can. If the activity is done outdoors, the object could be anything from a jungle gym to a square of pavement to a tree. Again, at the end of the observation time, have the kids share their observations with each other.

After your kids have done a single-object observation activity once or twice, they can expand the concept into writing simple poems that include something they observed and something of themselves:

> The bark of the tree is rough.
> I could scratch my back on it the way cows do.
> The leaves of the tree are like a green roof.
> I could make my house in it.
> The tree stays in the same place all the time.
> I could never be so still.
> The tree is taller than all the houses.
> If I climbed to the top I could see for miles.
> When I pull off a leaf it doesn't make a sound.
> I wonder if the tree feels anything.

The best-known model for this kind of poem is Wallace Stevens' "Thirteen Ways of Looking at a Blackbird." It may be too abstract for kids to get a real feel for, but you might try reading it to your kids along with the simpler model just given, and then suggest subjects for poems they might write—"10 Ways of Looking at a Yo-Yo," "99 Ways of Looking at a Brick," etc.

Stream-of-Consciousness Writing

There is another world to be observed besides the outer one the senses contact. It is, of course, the inner world of emotions, thoughts, instincts and impulses. The poet observes the details of that world as thoroughly as he does the details of the outer world. In fact, he often explores the two simultaneously, and the resulting poems are always a product of the meeting of those two worlds. The last part of the "Observation" activity in this chapter demonstrates this joining process to kids, as the poet chooses outer details and matches them with information from inside: "The tree is taller. . . ./If I climbed to the top. . . ."

This activity asks kids to pay close attention to what's happening inside them by doing stream-of-consciousness writing. They can do this by sitting quietly with their journals and recording everything that occurs to them. You'll probably notice that this is not at all easy for many kids to do at first. Some may say that they're not thinking of anything, that nothing's happening; others might complain that their writing can't keep up with the speed for their thoughts. For the slow starters, you might want to provide a model or two—you could even do an oral stream-of-consciousness demonstration, starting with "I'm not thinking of anything," or "Nothing's happening":

> Nothing's happening. I can't think of anything. My stomach is growling. I forgot to eat breakfast. I can't wait until lunch. My arm hurts. Julie's working hard and I can't think of anything. Her shoes are dirty. My feet feel really hot. I wish I could go barefoot. . . .

You can also give them some things to think about before they begin: Notice how you feel. Are you happy, angry, tired? Notice parts of your body. How do they feel? Notice other people and notice what you think about them. Notice what you think about when you look at different objects—rulers, books, lunch boxes. What do different objects remind you of?

For the kids who get frustrated because their writing doesn't keep up with the flow of their thoughts, tell them not to worry about it and just write as much as they can. Let them know that punctuation and correct spelling are not important in this activity, so they can dispense with those things if it helps them to write faster.

When all the kids have finished writing, make sure everyone gets the chance to read aloud what they've written. The activity can show children about themselves and about other people through the processes of awareness and reflection.

After a few classes have been devoted to stream-of-consciousness writing, most kids should feel at ease with it. Then you can encourage them to practice such writing on their own time, using the journals discussed earlier. You can also encourage them to turn their stream-of-consciousness writing into poems.

Nouns into Verbs

Language is always changing. Science and technology seem to give us new words almost daily—quasar, quark, lidar and on and on. Slang words, too, come and go. And we're always snatching words from other languages—for example, karma and nirvana from Sanskrit. Journalists and public figures often coin words that work their way into daily use. (President Harding once called for a return to "normalcy"—a word that still doesn't have a respectable place in dictionaries, but one that people use all the time. And back in the early '50s, a skimpy two-piece bathing suit appeared on the fashion scene at the same time the U.S. was testing hydrogen bombs in the South Pacific. Some journalists got together and named that new atomic-age bathing suit after the place where the nuclear tests were being held—Bikini Atoll.)

Meanings of words change too. In fact, words can come to mean just the opposite of what they first meant. Two or three hundred years ago, "awful" wasn't such an awful word—it meant "awesome," not "terrible." And "artificial" was a compliment meaning a significant achievement of artistry.

One of the ways people change language is by making nouns into verbs. This can be a particularly effective device for the poet to use if it's not done clumsily or too often. To get kids going on changing nouns into verbs, give them some examples from common usage: The dog treed the raccoon. What he said absolutely floored me! I'll chair the meeting. The younger generation mirrors the attitudes of its elders. The coach benched his goalie. The gardener potted his begonia.

Once they're familiar with the idea, ask your kids to turn any nouns they like into verbs and write definitions for them. Encourage them to be as outlandish as possible, to make verbs from such nouns as pajamas, volcano, garbage, linoleum, antenna and anything/everything else that comes to mind. Of course the new verbs can't mean just anything—they have to have some connection with the meaning of their noun parent, just as "mirrors" means to reflect, and "benched" means to make sit on the bench instead of playing.

When the kids have defined all their new verbs, they can write them into sentences, read them to the class and see if others can guess their meanings. Those they particularly like can be kept for use in their writings or put into their journal. (The poem on the cover of this book came from an assignment to write a poem that used a noun as a verb; in this case, "music" was the new verb.)

Making Similes and Metaphors

Central to almost all poetry is imagery. An image is a device that illuminates an experience, a feeling, an object or an idea by connecting it, or reconnecting it in a new way, to one of the five senses. It is constructed with similes and metaphors. A simile is a stated comparison using "like" or "as"—my love is like a city. A metaphor is an implied comparison that foregoes "like" and "as"—my heart is a whale. A good image works to expand the reader's perception of something, to help him see, hear, taste, touch or smell in a new way, or to experience or understand known ideas or emotions with new force. Here are a few particularly intriguing images:

"Raise the live rafters of the eardrum"—Dylan Thomas

"The great yellow days turning their spokes"—W.S. Merwin

"When the sky is a cellar/with dirty windows"—Denise Levertov

To get kids into writing similes and metaphors you can begin with a whole-class discussion and walk them through the process a few times. Here's a sample:

(Hold up a book)
Teacher: Tell me something about this book.
Kids: It's boring!

T: OK. How boring is it?

K: Very boring.

T: There's another way to say how boring it is and that's to compare it with something else that's boring and say, "This book is as boring as . . . ." What? What else is boring?

K: School.

T: Good. This book is as boring as school. What else?

K: When it's raining on Saturday and there's nothing to do.

T: Fine. This book is as boring as rainy Saturdays. These kinds of comparisons are an important part of poetry. They're called similes.

After going through this kind of discussion a few times, read the kids some poems that have similes in them and ask the kids to pick them out.

Similes are pretty easy to spot—they're comparisons that are commonly heard in everyday conversation. But metaphors usually are harder to grasp. Once again, the best way to start is to walk the class through the process of making images, this time using metaphors:

T: Let's talk about a feeling. How do you feel sometimes?

K: Happy. Mad. Sad.

T: OK, let's take mad. When you feel mad, what do you feel like doing?

K: Shouting at everybody. Fighting. Breaking stuff.

T: Can you think of anything that does those things, or things like them? That shouts or makes loud noises, that fights or hurts people, that breaks things?

K: A wild animal. A tornado. Dynamite.

T: Good. Now we can take all those words and make similes: I am as mad as a wild animal; I am as mad as a storm; I am as mad as dynamite. But we can also do something else. We can cross out "as mad as"— (write on the chalk board) I am *as mad as* dynamite—and what we have left is, I am dynamite. This is a special kind of comparison called a metaphor.

Once again, after doing this a few times, read your kids some poems with metaphors in them and ask the kids to pick out the metaphors.

When kids have a good sense of making metaphors, they can begin with a single metaphor and build a whole poem around it:

> T: Now we're going to make a poem using the metaphor "I am dynamite." What does dynamite do?
>
> K: Explodes.
>
> T: I am dynamite.
>   I explode.
>   What happens when dynamite explodes?
>
> K: It breaks glass. Splinters wood. Knocks down walls.
>
> T: I am dynamite.
>   I explode.
>   I break windows
>   and tear wood into splinters.
>   I knock down walls.
>   OK. What else about dynamite?
>
> K: It's very hot. Starts fires.
>
> T: I am dynamite.
>   I explode.
>   I break windows
>   and tear wood into splinters.
>   I knock down walls.
>   Everything burns in my heat.
>   What happens when it's finished?
>
> K: Everything is quiet. Ashes and dust in the air. Burning smell.
>
> T: I am dynamite.
>   I explode.
>   I break windows
>   and tear wood into splinters.
>   I knock down walls.
>   Everything burns in my heat.
>   Then everything is quiet.
>   Dust and ashes in the air.
>   The smell of burning.
>   OK. Now we have a small poem. Is it about dynamite?
>
> K: Yes.
>
> T: What else is it about? How did we start?
>
> K: About being mad.
>
> T: So what shall we call this poem?
>
> K: 'Being Mad.'

Finding appropriate and effective similes or metaphors is important for a poet. If an image is just right, the poet can explore all its possibilities and grow the poem directly from it, always checking with the central notion or sense of the poem—in the case of the dynamite poem, the center was anger—to see that there is a true fit. As kids learn to make their own similes and metaphors, they can write down and keep in their journals the ones they especially like.

Crazy Comparisons

The preceding activity dealt with comparisons—similes and metaphors. Effective comparisons, however, aren't easy to come by—red as a rose, white as snow and I am a rock just don't make it. Following is a list of 25 questions that asks kids to compare oddly matched pairs of things. The kids can answer the questions with a sentence or two or, even better, write poems that develop the comparisons. But the point here is more than just a few laughs; doing this activity can help kids learn how to look in the most unexpected places for comparisons, and that's what the working poet does all the time—all the expected comparisons have been used up and have gone to Cliché Heaven.

Here are the questions:

1. How is a laugh like a bowling ball?
2. How is a cloud like a watermelon?
3. How is a picture like a stomach ache?
4. How is anger like a floor?
5. How is music like a bed?
6. How is a giraffe like Sunday afternoon?
7. How is 5 o'clock like a shovel?
8. How is a table like a dream?
9. How is tomorrow like a piano?
10. How is breathing like a pencil?
11. How is school like spaghetti?
12. How is a harmonica like November?
13. How is a basket like a fire?
14. How is blood like a song?
15. How is a tree like a wish?
16. How is being scared like a wheel?
17. How is skin like a lie?
18. How is a street like the sun?
19. How is plastic like a sneeze?
20. How is an eraser like California?

21. How is a mountain like a nap?
22. How is a word like a ladybug?
23. How is a joke like a towel?
24. How is an idea like a necklace?
25. How is water like a memory?

Obviously the list could go on forever. So if none of these comparisons gets your kids going, ask them to make up their own in a class discussion, allowing plenty of time for them to create lots of odd comparisons.

Condensing A Long Story into A Poem

In general, a poem aims to convey the essence of an experience or an event rather than to describe it in all its particulars. Whereas the novelist or story writer may present a careful and thoroughly detailed account, the poet seeks out the one or the few definitive, central details that bring the reader right to the heart of the matter.

By turning stories into poems, kids not only can develop the ability to understand what feelings or ideas are at the center of complicated events and experiences, they can also get a finer sense of what poetry is all about and how it is different from stories and novels. This activity and the two that follow can help kids learn where to look for the poetic—where to find poems.

Before your kids try on their own to make stories into poems, let them have a go at it a few times as a whole class. You can start the process by reading your class a familiar story, then working with them to extract the necessary elements to create a poem. Here's what one class did with the story of Cinderella:

Cinderella
Beautiful and sad
Working too hard
Sleeping in ashes
No kindness for her
Only wicked words
She dreams of a ball
And her dream comes true
She forgets her sadness
Dancing with a prince
But her dream ends
And she sleeps in ashes again
Without her glass slipper she would wonder
'Was it all real?'

But she knows it was
And the prince comes to find her
And they leave together
Forever

Tell the kids they can work with any stories, including TV show plots and comic book situations, that they like. Once they begin doing this activity on their own, they can also go to their stream-of-consciousness writing (see the earlier activity) and make poems from some of that, again choosing the details that work best to convey the mood or the tone of feelings. They can also use stories they write themselves, doing the stories first, then going back to find the poems in them.

Looking for Poems in Ordinary Experiences

Most poems don't concern themselves with hugely dramatic events such as the Trojan War or the storming of the Winter Palace. Instead they are built upon events which, seen from the outside, may be considered pretty ordinary. What the poet sees and writes about, though, isn't from the outside, but from the inside of an event, where the life juices churn and flow. The poet quickens an event by presenting its essence. He makes it his business to notice particular though perhaps not unusual moments of beauty, and to convey those moments so they come alive for the reader.

One thing kids learning about poetry need to cultivate is the ability to find and convey the interesting, unusual, striking, dramatic qualities of the ordinary events of daily life. The surest way to develop that ability is to read a lot of poetry, paying attention to how the poet brings everyday events to life. The poetry of William Carlos Williams is particularly good for learning about this skill because it uses plain, direct language and a simple style that won't baffle young readers.

To help your kids understand how a poet turns ordinary experiences into poems, ask them to work backward—have them read a poem first, then write a story-type narration of the event. Two William Carlos Williams poems, "So much depends" and "This is just to say," both of which are included in Williams' Selected Poems, listed in the resource section, will provide good material. If one were writing about "So much depends," for instance, he might say "I walked out into the farmyard after the rain stopped and I saw how wonderful the red wheelbarrow looked all wet and shiny, and how beautiful its red looked next to the white of the chickens standing beside it." A whimsical model that can provide great insight into this activity is L. Frank Baum's *Mother Goose in Prose*, in which he makes familiar nursery rhymes into stories with a lot of "behind-the-scenes" details.

Once kids have worked backwards from poem to event several times, they will probably have some sense of how a poet works from event to poem; then they can try it themselves. Offer the children a list of subjects—brushing teeth, eating cereal, taking a bath, going to the grocery store, riding a bicycle, talking with friends—and let them write freely, using Williams' poems in particular as a guide. Remind the kids to identify what they feel is particular or special about the event, to identify especially vivid details—the way the toothbrush sounds inside your head, the way the splash of water sounds against porcelain, the colors of packages, the feel of wind or the sound of wheels—and then build their poems around those details.

Found Poems

Michaelangelo said of his sculpting that there were beautiful figures inside his blocks of marble and that all he did was chip away chunks and bits here and there to release them. In much the same way, as the two preceding activities demonstrate, there is poetry inside blocks of events, and often what a poet does is strip away the non-essential elements in order to reveal a poem.

"Found poems" are ones that are made by using words someone else has written in another form and arranging them in lines of poetry. Kids can use words from almost anything—cereal boxes, newspapers, soft-drink cans, freeway signs, bulletin boards, graffiti—and arrange them as they like to make a poem. Here's one a natural foods-minded student made from the words found on several food packages:

> "Food"*
> sodium nitrate
> mouth-watering
> BHA
> savory
> monosodium glutamate
> spicy
> sodium nitrate

*In this and subsequent poems, you will note that there is a lack of capitalization. It is the poet's prerogative to choose the style and format for his poetry, and these do not always adhere to standard grammatical and punctuation rules.

delicious
fumaric acid
tart
sodium benzoate
the best you've ever tasted

Encourage your class to create a variety of "found poems" on any number of topics; they can be silly, serious, informative, instructive. The idea here is the leaner the better.

Memorization

Memorization has gotten a bad name. Many people associate it with old-fashioned school-masterish rigidity and adherence to a notion of education by rote. There are plenty of adults around who still squirm when they recall being made to memorize "The Wreck of the Hesperus" or "Evangeline." Yet the fact is that kids memorize all the time. In particular, they memorize songs; and they seem to do it because they like it. It's pretty clear, certainly, that it's not the fact of memorization that's odious, it's what students have been asked to memorize.

Memorization should be part of any work with poetry, because by memorizing something one comes to live with it, and one's appreciation and understanding of it deepens the more it becomes a part of him. If nothing else, kids should memorize some of their own poems. Beyond that, you might encourage them to pick out a few poems they like that others have written, and memorize them. If the kids are able to choose their own poems, memorization will be much more fun and much less ponderous.

Besides being a way of internalizing poetry, memorization can teach kids a lot about what poetry is. Originally, of course, poetry was spoken, not written, performed and passed on by recitation. Many poetic devices, rhyme in particular, came into being as aids to recitation. Kids will discover right away that rhyming poems are almost always easier to memorize than nonrhyming ones, and that lines with alliteration come easier to mind than lines without. But instead of pointing out these facts to your students, encourage class discussion on memorization by asking the kids about poems that they've memorized—which ones were easy, which difficult; which lines they tend to forget or misquote and why they think that happens.

Since poetry reciting can make a great performance, it may be just as pleasing to many kids to learn and recite poems as it is to play or dance in a recital or act in a play. You might like to set aside one or more full writing periods for students to recite poems they've learned, or make it a policy to give a few minutes of each writing period to students who have poems they want to recite. If enough kids enjoy reciting poetry, poetry performances could be scheduled during which kids read their own poems and recite poems they've memorized, inviting parents and friends to attend.

When kids are picking poems to memorize, encourage them to look for poems that everybody's not familiar with so they can share something new with the class. Each student will need to develop his or her own memorization techniques. Sometimes it's easiest to learn rhyming poems simply by reading them over and over again. Nonrhyming poems may take more methodical line-by-line memorization.

Looking for Poems

"What should I write about?" Though working poets don't normally ask that question of anyone but themselves, they do ask it, over and over again. Kids, of course, ask it too; they ask Teacher. This chapter includes 11 activities that you can use as assignments in poetry writing classes. Some of the activities provide specific subjects for poems, others suggest types and forms.

Most often, of course, poems don't come from assignments—they come from a poet's vision of himself and the world. One of the goals of any writing program ought to be to free student writers from a need for assignments, to get them to trust and use their abilities and responses to discover and make poems on their own. Writing assignments should be seen only as starters, stimuli that get kids working but are finally expendable.

All the writing activities in this chapter, even the more unusual ones like "Scenarios for Animated Films" and "Recipes," ask you and your students to work at making real poems. That doesn't mean your kids can't write witty or funny poems for these assignments; it does mean that they should try to get beyond what is simply silly and into poems with some thought and depth.

Being An Animal or An Object

When a starfish eats a mussel, it doesn't pry the shell open. It wraps itself tightly around the mussel and works its stomach into it through a small opening in the mussel's shell. When a poet writes about anything other than himself, he uses his imagination the way a starfish uses its stomach; he works it into his subject and digests what is at the center. His poems come from being "inside" another creature or object.

Many Native American peoples felt a spiritual affinity with animals and objects in their environments—more than an affinity, in fact, a feeling of identity so strong that they took their names from them—Sitting Bull, Crazy Horse, Black Elk, Red Cloud—and developed special relationships with them. Native American poetry is replete with poems and songs that sing of animals, trees, rocks, the sky. Shaking the Pumpkin, noted in the resource list of this book, is an anthology of Native American poetry filled with examples of this kind of poem. (Technicians of the Sacred, an anthology of poetry of aboriginal peoples from many parts of the world, also in the resource list, shows that the spiritual connection with nature wasn't exclusively Native American.)

A good writing exercise your class can try is writing poems about being animals or objects, speaking from "inside," trying to express the special quality or qualities of whatever it is they're writing about. These poems are difficult to write well. The danger is that the students won't really get inside, that instead they will posture and comment without conveying any sense of animal-ness or object-ness. Urge your kids to be simple and direct in their work. Ask them to write only about what they have a strong sense of, using observations first and intuition second. Warn them against the natural tendency to sentimentalize or trivialize—"It's tough to be a rock"; "I'd rather be a bird than a person." Also, let them know their poem shouldn't shift in and out of the animal or object, but should stay centered inside. An animal wouldn't speak about what it's like to be an animal, but would speak about what it feels and does. The same with any object. What your poets should try to understand is the special kind of consciousness a deer or a log might have. Here's a poem about a dancing bear you can use as a model:

> dancing bear
> man is everywhere i can smell him his clothes his food
> it is dark
> they have turned on the bright lights
> i am made to walk upright
> even now after all these years i give in
> to the urge to drop down onto all four legs
> the man yanks my strap
> slaps me sharply on the snout
> and i stand back up

i sit on a chair the way men do
music plays
i get up and turn around around
one after another the lights burn into my eyes
the people behind them laugh

the music changes
and i change what i do
balancing atop a huge ball
twice i fall
twice the man jerks hard on my strap
and whispers angrily
though his smile doesn't change
the third time i stay up
and walk the ball across the ring

now he starts a motorcycle
i straddle it and ride without my strap
it took me two years
to learn this

the music stops
i climb to a tightrope
and make my way across it slowly slowly
a cold wind riffles the hair on my back
i am high enough to see past the lights
up into the sky
i find the moon
it has gone everywhere with me

the people roar louder than engines
we stand facing them
he bows low

Besides the preceding poem and the poems in *Shaking the Pumpkin* and *Technicians of the Sacred,* you can look to the poetry of Ted Hughes for some models, particularly in his collection *Crow,* noted in the resource list.

Metamorphosis
The poet is an alchemist. He can change one thing into another with a few strokes of his pen. The first activity asks kids to write poems from the point of view of animals or objects. This activity

involves expressing the process of changing from one thing into another—from Dr. Jekyll into Mr. Hyde, from Joe Citizen into werewolf, from a flower into a book, from a shoe into a piano and on and on. Explain to your kids when they work on this exercise that their poems should pay attention to the physical structures of the things they're writing about—what happens to the person or thing, how it feels as the transformation takes place—rather than simply describing the change. Here's a poem about a man who changes into a bear:

> *finding the bathroom in a department store in downtown*
> *duluth*
> as you walk down the long flight of stairs
> you feel upheavals inside your body
> your skin grows coarse brown hair
> huge new muscles cleave to your bones
> thoughts drop away from your mind
>
> in the basement you cause panic
> customers scream parents clutch children
> strong men run and hide
>
> you laugh and shout
> what is this? what is this that's happening to me?
>
> you run and roar and crash into counters bellowing
> protect your wives
> i'll eat your children alive
>
> when everyone has fled
> you find the bathroom
> lock the door turn off the lights
> and lie down on the cool tile
> it is quiet
> you breathe big chunks of air
>
> your senses are sharp
> you can hear the sound of the city holding to the ground
> in your blood you feel the tug of the moon
>
> you stay still several minutes
> remembering things you never knew—
> the taste of grubs

79

the smell of winter's coming
a cold shiver runs up your back
you move like a glacier
out the door
upstairs
to where your family waits
you gather them up
outside the city has disappeared
you travel fast now in pure light
your children fall asleep clinging to your back
you lick the fur on your mate's neck

Photos

Whatever else the poet seems to be writing about, he's always writing about himself as well—his own particular vision of the world. Lots of poetry may not seem to be autobiographical when in fact it really is. Other poetry is quite apparently the poet examining and singing about himself and his life.

Kids generally seem to enjoy talking about their past; they seem to like hearing stories from parents and other relatives about what they did when they were younger; they like to look at pictures of themselves in the family album. You can help turn that interest into poetry.

Ask each student to bring to class several snapshots of himself from various times in his life, and then write a poem about himself that relates to each picture. The poems that work best are generally dramatic monologues—the person in the picture speaking the poem directly in the first person, rather than a third person poet speaking about the person in the picture. When each poem is done to his satisfaction, the poet can mount the appropriate picture at the top of a page—perhaps in his journal—and write the poem under it.

The demand in this exercise is that kids really use their imaginations to try to feel and speak what their younger selves would be feeling and speaking. They might try to connect their poems with an important event in their lives that occurred around the time the picture was taken, such as a vacation, the first day of school or a special holiday. The kids should try to capture the sense, the tone, the mood of being the age they were when the picture was taken. What did they like to do then? What were they afraid of? What made them happy and sad? Who were their friends? What did they want to do that they couldn't? You can suggest these and other questions for them to ponder while composing their poems.

This activity can also work well with photos of other family members. By writing in the first person, the students will have to do the imaginative work of trying to understand what it feels like to be another person—something the working poet is trying to do all the time.

Concrete Poems and Shaped Poems

Both concrete poems and shaped poems use the placement of words on a page to create an effect. The difference between them is that shape is central to concrete poetry's effect—the words of a concrete poem written in regular poetic lines would mean little or nothing at all as poetry. In shaped poetry, however, the poem can stand on its own words; the shape it takes isn't essential but it does heighten the poem's effect.

At its present stage of development, concrete poetry is still a slight genre—and it may always be so. Even the best concrete poems normally lack real force, intensity or impact. They are more like verbal/visual amusements, more witty than powerful, more interesting than illuminating, but most kids who try making them like them because they can be so funny and unusual. There are two books on concrete poetry in the resource list—*Concrete Poetry* and *Anthology of Concrete Poetry*—that can provide models. You can use these or others to stimulate your students' own creations.

Shaped poetry is more common and more forceful than concrete poetry; the idea here is to arrange line lengths so that the poem will create a picture, as in this poem called "Mountain":

to
hear what
mountains hear:
humming of granite,
low growl of basalt, old
thin whine of silver singing
back and back into itself: many
musics of earth's holding together

May Swenson has written a book of shaped poems called *Iconography*, listed in the resource section. You can use some of the poems in it as more models for your kids.

Scenarios for Animated Films

There's a large and growing group of animated film makers who don't adhere to the Disney line. The films they make are often plotless, with fantastical images flowing in and out of each other, with illogical (or metalogical) sequences and dream-like metamorphoses of objects into other objects. They are, in a very real sense, visual poems.

This activity doesn't ask students to use a camera to make an animated film. All that's needed is pencil and paper to write a scenario. Students should pretend to write a film as it would be seen, making simple declarative statements as though they were instructions to the film maker.

After you show your class the two following models, turn them loose on this activity with encouragement to be as wild and crazy as they can be.

> Poem 1
> as a man stands on a street corner
> waiting for a green light
> his bones leave him
> leaving him
> a puddle
> he looks at the holes in peoples' shoes for awhile
> chuckling
> but soon grows tired of that
> he grows irritable
> smokes several packs of cigarettes
> hollers at children who try to splash on him
> hisses at dogs and cats who try to lap him up
>
> winter comes
> and ice forms on him
> he tries to shout the ice off
> but the only sounds he can make are tinkley
> and far away
> just then a cab screeches to a stop beside him
> and his bones get out
> we're sorry we left
> they say
> it's a cold cruel world out there
> the man gets together with his bones
> and when the light turns green
> he walks away
>
> Poem 2
> at a birthday party for a king

someone gives him the deed to a small country
out of his birthday cake
pop all the people from the king's new country
they bow down
and take off their shoes
and flow out of the bottoms of their clothes
into a bowl on the floor
the king takes off his robes
revealing that he is an eggbeater
he gets into the bowl
and beats the mass into a stiff meringue
a platoon of mounted sculptors arrives
they shape the meringue
into a statue of the king
playing a cello

Dream Poems

Like the animated films discussed in the previous activity, dreams
also seem to be the natural stuff of poetry. Without getting Freudian
or Jungian, you can suggest to your kids that they try to remember
their dreams—perhaps keep a note pad by their bed and write the
dreams down as soon as they wake up in the morning—and then
turn them into poems.

Dream poems shouldn't include any comments by the poet, just
what happened in the dream. And the poet can be selective. He
doesn't need to include every detail, but can choose the important
or vivid ones that give an accurate feeling for what the dream was
like. Remind your students that there's no need to "make sense,"
since in everyday logical terms, few dreams make sense. The real
sense dreams do make are the feelings that grow from them, and it's
those feelings kids' dream poems should convey. An eighth grader
wrote the following dream poem, which you can show your kids as
a model:

I am sitting in a chair
watching television.
A man comes in the window.
I am the man.
He stabs me in the back
and all my blood flows out of the wound
making a big puddle on the floor.
Silver frogs jump out of the puddle
take me by the hands

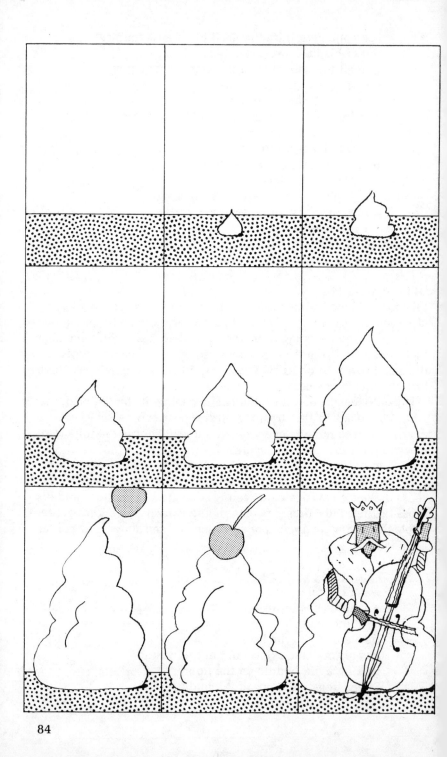

and pull me down into it.
It is a beautiful clear lake.
I am a fish
but I talk with a human voice.

Myth Poems

The myths we know offer explanations of the beginnings of things—how the earth came to be, how humankind appeared, where the sun came from and so on. Myths appeal to that part of us that scientific reasoning can't touch; the myth is a poetic, emotional, spiritual expression, not a rational one.

Myths and poetry go hand in hand, and you can combine the two in this writing assignment. First, read your class some myths— Roman, Greek, Scandinavian, aboriginal—then have the kids write their own myth poems. Topics could be: Where did the wind come from? Why do we die? What are dreams? Why don't trees walk? Where did the mountains come from? Explain to your students that their myths are to be poems, not stories, and that they needn't get involved in long narrative detail; the myth poems should contain a few vivid, interesting details that can carry the sense of the work and the story along. Here's a myth poem about where the sound of the sea came from:

> the god of lions
> drunk one night
> dropped some lions
> into
> the green ocean
> instead of africa
> delighting the god of oceans
> who wouldn't let them go
> now
> lonesome for their home
> they roar
> and roar

Recipes

A good way to get your young poets cooking is to have them write recipe poems—not the Betty Crocker kind, but outlandish recipes for dishes that aren't a normal part of anybody's diet. Leaf loaf. Cloud soup. Airplane sandwiches. Star pudding. Obviously, recipe poems can be comical, but they don't necessarily have to be. The tone, in fact, can be quite serious:

Rock Pie
Use only
the ripest stones.
Fresh ones ring
when you hit them,
old ones thud.
Put a pie crust on a window sill
where moonlight falls
and put the stones
beside it.
Forget about them.
One night
when everything is just right
the stones will jump
into the crust
and the pie will be ready.
If the stones haven't moved
after a hundred years
get some new ones
and try again.

Star Bread (a cinquain)
Put stars
In a clay bowl.
Add wheat and a river.
Mix. Form loaves. They will bake themselves.
Slice them.

Haiku

Too many poetry teachers have loved the haiku nearly to death. They think they can gather words describing trees, grass, lakes and stars, slap them together and get a good haiku. Wrong. When haiku is practiced by masters, the effect can be tremendously forceful and moving. But when haiku is practiced by those who don't really understand it, the results are often cute, sweet and terrible.

This isn't to say, Don't teach haiku. It is to say, Teach it properly. You can begin by reading some books that discuss haiku and contain good examples of it (see the resource list). Then you can select several examples from the books to use for models for your kids' writing.

Your class will need to know the technical details about haiku. Haiku are written in three lines using seventeen syllables—five in the first line, seven in the second line and five in the third. The

poems always deal with nature, focusing on small details of the natural world rather than on grand panoramas. And they are always written in the present tense to give a sense of both immediacy and transience.

Beyond these technical details, you can explain, haiku aren't purely and simply nature poems; they also are meant to reveal— not to *say* but to *reveal*—the poet's mood or emotions, through writing about nature. As obvious examples, a leaf falling off a tree in autumn could suggest sadness, reflections on mortality; sprouting grass in springtime might suggest joyful vigor, hope.

Your kids probably won't master the form right away. But it will help them immensely if they know what it's all about, and what they should be striving to achieve.

Cinquains

Free verse isn't always freeing for young writers—some often prefer to write in rather strict forms. Strict structure gives kids a framework to fit words into, and it has a kind of puzzle-solving quality that kids seem to like.

One form that is strict but simple is the cinquain. The cinquain is a five-line poem with two syllables in the first line, four syllables in the second line, six in the third, eight in the fourth and two again in the fifth. Because it's such a short poem, each word must be carefully chosen for maximum effect. In most cases the writer doesn't overload the poem with articles, since they gobble up syllables that could be saved for more striking words.

To teach your class about this tight poetry form, read or write on the board some model cinquains, showing the students the 2-4-6-8-2 syllable formula. Then have the class as a group write a cinquain and, finally, have kids work individually on some of their own. Here are some models you can use:

> *Swimming at Night*
> White moon.
> Cry of a loon.
> Diving through the cold black,
> Touching the ancient lake bottom—
> Fish teeth.

> *Winter Morning*
> Breakfast
> Sunny kitchen
> The smell of hot coffee

Buckwheat cakes and blackberry jam
Cold milk

A Brand-new Form

If your kids enjoy writing within structured forms, there's no reason why they shouldn't experiment with forms they invent themselves. Before you set them loose to do this, though, try to acquaint them with various existing forms to give them some ideas about the new kinds they can create.

The cinquain and the haiku are composed of a specific number of lines and syllables. There's another old Japanese form called "waka" that is also written to a specific formula: five lines and 31 syllables—5,7,5,7,7. When your class begins to invent new forms, encourage them to start with forms that specify lines and syllables. For instance, they could try a 10-line poem with one syllable in the first line, two syllables in the second line, three in the third and so on. Or they could write a poem of ten lines with syllable restrictions of 1,2,3,4,5,5,4,3,2,1. There aren't any rules for creating forms. Anything goes.

There are other more complicated poetry forms that can also provide models for kids' inventions. The sestina is one. It's a 7-stanza, 39-line poem. At the end of every one of the first 36 lines (six stanzas) comes one of six words the poet decided upon beforehand. The words are to occur in this order—123456 615243 364125 532614 451362 246531. The final stanza of the sestina is three lines long and each line contains two of the six end words— the first line has words 1 and 2, the second line 3 and 4 and the third line 5 and 6. Kids can fiddle with the sestina form and come up with their own variations of recurring end words. They could use three words, for instance, 123 312 231. In addition to the sestina, other forms may also stimulate variations—the limerick, for example, or the sonnet.

After a class writing period in which you discuss the various structured forms and show how new ones might be made, ask your kids to try to create some of their own. When a student invents a new form, he could explain it to the class, and then ask everyone to write a poem in that style.

EPILOGUE

If kids are to learn about making poetry, they need to do more than just write poems—they need responses to what they've written. We feel that an appropriate response is not a grade of A,B,C,D or F. Nor are a few swift comments—"Good"; "Needs work here"; "I don't understand"—scribbled on a page particularly helpful. The best way for student poets to learn from what they've done is to get comments on their work from a critique group of fellow poets.

A critique group may be composed of all the class members or just a few students. The group's function is to listen to and respond to poems presented to it. Any writer who has a poem to present can read it to the group. Group members then respond to the poem not by saying "good" or "bad" but by considering such questions as, How did the poem make you feel? What words, phrases, images, lines were particularly effective? What feeling or experience was the poet trying to express? What did you understand and not understand? How could the poet improve the poem? The group should discuss the poem while the writer remains silent and listens. After a few minutes the poet can join in, answering criticisms, asking for suggestions, etc.

After the poet has received peer responses to his poem, what then? He may choose to ignore everything and leave his poem as is. He may also feel he's discovered ways to improve it. Try to encourage your kids to consider revision an important part of making poems—some poets say it's the most important thing they do. If kids are to grow as writers, they must learn to recognize weaknesses in what they write, to improve what doesn't work well, to clarify, hone and polish.